# *the*
# BASEBALL
# BOOK *of*
# WHY

### THE ANSWERS TO QUESTIONS
### YOU'VE ALWAYS WONDERED
### ABOUT FROM AMERICA'S
### NATIONAL PASTIME

## JOHN McCOLLISTER, PHD

LYONS
PRESS

Guilford, Connecticut

An imprint of The Rowman & Littlefield Publishing Group, Inc.
4501 Forbes Blvd., Ste. 200
Lanham, MD 20706
www.rowman.com

Distributed by NATIONAL BOOK NETWORK

British Library Cataloguing in Publication Information available
Library of Congress Control Number: 2019957519

ISBN 978-1-4930-4887-8 (paperback)
ISBN 978-1-4930-4888-5 (e-book)

# Introduction

"Why?"

That tiny, seemingly innocent word has driven people, even nations, to examine the reasons we began the traditions we accept as a normal part of our lives.

Fans of baseball know this all too well.

Yet, modern-day enthusiasts of what has been deemed America's Pastime are not always of the same opinion as to why some tradition may have begun. Loyalties are often dictated by the team for which they cheered as youngsters. High-powered business executives wear replicas of team jerseys to an important meeting on Wall Street. Teens wear T-shirts spelling out in bold print a particular ball club.

One thing that unites them all, however, is an appreciation of the sport that begat these traditions.

That's what this book is all about.

Some of the answers to these questions, each of which begins with that intriguing word "why" are brief and to the point. Others require more detail in order to give a meaningful response.

Whatever the case, this writer hopes that each question and answer in this volume will allow the reader to appreciate, even more, the greatest sport ever created.

# Acknowledgments

No book is ever written in a vacuum. I relied on friends of baseball without whose help the production of this volume would have been impossible.

Special thanks goes to Pittsburgh-based marketing and public relations consultant Todd Miller for editing and fact-checking this manuscript.

Thanks also to Rick Rinehart of Rowman and Littlefield for his guidance and support throughout the creative stages of this project. You are the absolute greatest.

# WHY DO WE SOMETIMES REFER TO A LEFT-HANDED PITCHER AS A "SOUTHPAW"?

Baseball announcers as well as other fans of the game, perhaps in an attempt to insert an extra dimension of variety into the broadcast, will sometimes refer to the pitcher on the mound as a "southpaw" if he's a left-handed thrower. The reason is quite simple once you think about it.

Baseball stadiums are designed to have batters looking east or northeast. When a pitcher faces the batter, he receives the sign from the catcher and prepares to toss the pitch, be it a fastball, a curveball, or even a knuckler, with his body facing west. As a result, the left side of his body as well as his left arm are facing south. When the pitcher eventually lets go of the ball, he's releasing it from the south side of the mound.

Hence, he's called a "southpaw."

Get it?

# WHY ARE MAJOR LEAGUE BASEBALL PITCHERS NORMALLY LIMITED TO 100 PITCHES PER GAME?

Throughout Major League Baseball, as well as within the minor and amateur leagues, when a pitcher on the mound nears the 100 mark in the total of his tosses, his manager, in all probability, will have notified his bullpen to alert one of the relief pitchers to prepare to enter the contest.

The reason is that most physical therapists and other medical experts are of the opinion that an athlete's arm will endure this much strain before showing signs of fatigue.

Of course there are exceptions to this practice. One rather stunning example in modern times happened on July 2, 1963, in San Francisco's Candlestick Park when the Giants hosted the visiting Milwaukee Braves.

Neither team was setting the world ablaze, despite the fact that both squads featured some future Hall of Famers. The visiting Braves had the likes of Henry Aaron, Eddie

Mathews, and Warren Spahn. San Francisco heralded Willie Mays, Orlando Cepeda, and Juan Marichal.

The aging Spahn (42 years old) no longer had his overpowering fastball, but he had developed a wicked curveball that left opposing hitters shaking their heads in awe and disbelief after seeing a third strike nip the lower outside corner of the plate.

His mound opponent, 25-year-old Marichal, was no slouch himself. In only his fourth year of big-league baseball, this high-kicking native of the Dominican Republic eschewed finesse to keep hitters off-balance with an overpowering fastball.

Both pitchers wasted no time in setting down their opponents in order in the first. And so it continued throughout the night as the temperature dipped below 60 degrees.

At the conclusion of regulation time, both pitchers said they could go on.

In spite of the rather cool temperature, most of the 15,921 fans in attendance stayed to watch what they anticipated was developing into a classic pitchers' duel. Following each inning most of the sleepy-eyed fans rose and applauded to show their appreciation.

Each of the two pitchers waited for the other to blink.

But neither Spahn nor Marichal made a habit of blinking.

At 12:21 a.m., in the bottom of the 16th inning, after Harvey Kuenn grounded out, up to the plate stepped a heretofore hitless Mays. The Giants' superstar swung at Spahn's first pitch and smacked a towering fly ball to deep left-center field. The hometown crowd screamed with delight as they watched the ball disappear over the fence and into the chilly morning air.

The Giants won the game 1–0. But other numbers stood out more than the score: Marichal that night threw 227 pitches and Spahn, 201.

Those in attendance would not need any printed box score to remember the most important thing: they were fortunate to see one of the greatest baseball games ever played.

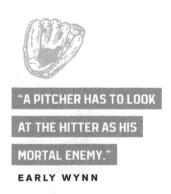

**"A PITCHER HAS TO LOOK AT THE HITTER AS HIS MORTAL ENEMY."**

**EARLY WYNN**

# WHY WAS JACK ROOSEVELT ROBINSON THE FIRST AFRICAN AMERICAN EVER TO PLAY AS PART OF AN OFFICIAL TEAM LINEUP IN MAJOR LEAGUE BASEBALL?

Any baseball historian knows that Jack (the name he preferred, as opposed to "Jackie") Robinson, of the old Brooklyn Dodgers, was the first person of color to be invited to join a Major League Baseball club.

Other talented ballplayers had aspirations of filling this designation in history, many of whom were relegated to teams in the so-called Negro League. But, according to many observers, there were three specific reasons why Robinson eventually was the one selected.

1) He brought fans to the field. The Brooklyn Dodgers suffered in attendance figures. While Ebbets Field was the site of a significant number of memorable moments, team records in the mid-1940s were mediocre. On Opening Day of 1947, April 15, Robinson's first official day in a Dodger uniform, 26,623 fans were in attendance (of the potential

32,000 capacity), and an estimated 14,000 of them were African Americans.

2) America needed a sports leader to help conquer racial prejudice. The last struggle of the Civil War did not squelch unjustified attacks on black citizens; in some areas they only escalated. Signs throughout the nation spelled out in bold print "White" or "Colored." Everyone knew the rules. Robinson had the education, character, and fortitude to withstand the abuse that would come with breaking them.

3) The persuasive power of Branch Rickey was overwhelming. Everyone knew that Major League Baseball had imposed a "whites only" policy on all of its owners. Two years after the 1944 death of then commissioner Judge Landis, his replacement was the former Kentucky governor and US senator Albert B. "Happy" Chandler. Self-proclaimed experts were confident that this "good ole' Southern country boy" would maintain the tradition of the past.

Those experts were wrong.

Chandler was convinced that the times were changing. He felt that if black men were willing to give their lives in World War II, which had ended less than three years earlier, then they should certainly be welcome to give their service to baseball.

With the support of Rickey, the general manager and part owner of the Dodgers, Chandler permitted the signing of a superb African American athlete out of UCLA named Jackie Robinson.

JACKIE ROBINSON IN 1954.

One of the first tasks Rickey accepted was to invite Robinson into a closed-door meeting in his office to set some informal ground rules that included something like this admonition: "I don't need just a colored player. . . . If a runner slides into you if you're covering second base and calls you a 'black son-of-a bitch,' I need a man who will have the courage *not* to fight back."

Robinson spent the 1946 season with the minor-league Montreal Royals, where he batted .349 and swiped 40 bases, and he was invited to join the Dodgers at their spring training camp in Daytona Beach.

Not all of his new teammates welcomed him with open arms. Fred "Dixie" Walker was one of the more outspoken critics and demanded to be traded. His club shortly thereafter sold him to the last-place Pittsburgh Pirates. Others, such as another "Southern boy," Harold "Pee Wee" Reese, became close friends and loyal supporters of Robinson throughout his career.

On that memorable April 15, the entire baseball world focused on Brooklyn's Ebbets Field when Jack Roosevelt Robinson crossed the white foul line to take his position at first base.

"BASEBALL IS LIKE A POKER GAME. NOBODY WANTS TO QUIT WHEN HE'S LOSING; NOBODY WANTS YOU TO QUIT WHEN YOU'RE AHEAD."

JACKIE ROBINSON

# WHY IS A BASEBALL FIELD SOMETIMES REFERRED TO AS A DIAMOND?

The average fan knows that every baseball infield has 90 feet between bases. It would seem, therefore that the equal distances would form a square. Not so.

Two theories became the source of this conclusion: One school of thought says that the framers of our national sport moved second base a few inches closer to home plate in order to make it slightly easier for a catcher to throw-out a runner attempting to steal second. The second theory is that while standing in the batter's box, a player would get a slightly different view of the infield. Because of an optical illusion, both the first and third bases appeared to be somewhat closer than 90 feet. With second base moved slightly infield, the position of the bases would reflect the shape of the gem that symbolizes a life of holy matrimony.

# WHY ARE THE PITTSBURGH PIRATES NAMED AFTER CRIMINALS WHO SAILED ON THE HIGH SEAS?

At first, it might seem strange for any franchise to adopt the name of those who gained a reputation as feared terrorists among otherwise honest, hardworking sailors who braved the normal perils of rough seas, unpredictable winds, and other threats to mind and body. It's a lot easier to comprehend once you know the complete story.

In 1890, the teams considered to be the "major leagues" of that era were faring quite well. To the dismay of the majority of the players, however, the team owners were pocketing most of the profits. Complaints from the players grew increasingly louder. By the end of the season, the majority of those wearing a team uniform—including those of the Pittsburgh Alleghenys (the adopted spelling of that era)—elected to form their own organization and call themselves the Players' League.

Perhaps due to lack of management skills, the new league lasted only one year. When the players sought to return to their former venues, even they were amazed that their former owners welcomed them back.

One of the better players—infielder Louis Bierbauer—thought he would return to his old team, the Philadelphia Athletics. Due to a clerical error, his name was accidentally left off the list of those who were eligible to return.

That error was caught by the new Pittsburgh club president, J. Patrick O'Neil, who persuaded Bierbauer to join the Alleghenys. Bierbauer agreed.

The Philadelphia team cried foul.

THE 1909 NATIONAL LEAGUE CHAMPION PITTSBURGH PIRATES DEPICTED AS, WELL, PIRATES.

Following heated discussions by both teams, the issue was submitted to binding arbitration.

The Pittsburgh franchise prevailed.

The Philadelphia Athletics protested the decision of the arbitrator. A representative for the club told a group of reporters that, in his opinion, Pittsburgh's signing of Bierbauer was "piratical."

That one accusation, designed to be an insult, had just the opposite effect. It became, instead, a badge of pride. Hence, from 1891 to this day, the Pittsburgh Baseball Club proudly adopted as its team name "the Pirates."

"SOME DAYS YOU TAME THE TIGER,
AND SOME DAYS THE TIGER HAS
YOU FOR LUNCH."

TUG MCGRAW

# WHY DID BASEBALL FANS IN PITTSBURGH DELIGHT TO HEAR THE ANNOUNCER CALL UPON A FICTIONAL "AUNT MINNIE" DURING GAMES?

One of the genuine characters among the legion of baseball announcers throughout the history of radio broadcasting was Albert Kennedy "Rosey" Rowswell, a diminutive (5-foot-6, 120-pound) play-by-play man from 1936 to 1955.

Over these years, this colorful announcer developed a unique vocabulary to describe the action on the field. But in many instances, unless you were a resident of Pittsburgh, you might need an interpreter to translate what he said. For example, when an opposing batter struck out, it was an "old dipsy doodle." If a Pirate got an extra-base hit, it was a "doozey marooney." There were many more. Out-of-towners who were new to Pirate broadcasts had to get used to this different jargon.

Rosey's most famous description was for a home run hit by a Pirate. Whenever a slugger such as Ralph Kiner would launch a mighty homer high over the scoreboard in left field, Rosey would shout into the microphone, "Raise the window, Aunt Minnie! Here it comes, right into your petunia patch!" After a pause of about two seconds, he would sigh, "She never made it. She never made it."

There was, of course, no petunia patch. And Aunt Minnie was a fictional character. But to Pittsburgh fans of that generation, this didn't matter. She was a welcome part of every family.

"NEVER LET THE FEAR OF STRIKING OUT KEEP YOU FROM COMING TO BAT."

**BABE RUTH**

# WHY DID CHICAGO'S WRIGLEY FIELD NOT HOST NIGHT GAMES UNTIL LONG AFTER WORLD WAR II?

Chicago's Wrigley Field is one of the oldest Major League Baseball fields, but it was unable to host night games until 1988 simply because until that time it contained no lights.

This is not to imply that nighttime baseball was a welcome addition to the MLB schedule. The reason for its inclusion to the American sporting scene was added revenue. Initial reaction was essentially negative. Detroit owner Frank Navin labeled night games "the beginning of the end of Major League Baseball." Ed Barrow, general manager of the Yankees, felt they would become "a wart on the nose of the game."

Logic eventually won the battle of words. Night baseball would allow far more fans to see games after work. By the end of the 1941 season, 9 of the 14 major-league teams had installed lights.

Chicago Cubs owner Philip Wrigley had reluctantly scheduled the installation of light towers to begin on

WRIGLEY FIELD AT NIGHT.

December 8, 1941. However, the "Day of Infamy" scuttled those plans.

Following the war, residents of the area opposed the installation of lights and the traffic jams that were bound to occur as a result of night games. Almost four decades later, Governor Jim Thompson signed into law a bill prohibiting the use of lights at the ballpark. In fact, the Cubs remained the last holdouts and did not host their first night game until 1988.

Today, the majority of Major League Baseball games are played after dark. Experts agree that, as a result, attendance is much greater than it would be if contests were still limited to the hours of sunshine.

# WHY ARE MODERN PLAYERS EXPECTED TO BE A CERTAIN HEIGHT IN ORDER TO PLAY BIG-LEAGUE BASEBALL?

While there is no official requirement that a big-league baseball player be of a certain height or weight (or gender) in order to make a team roster, the criteria for admission include the approval of the commissioner.

This became a concern back in the early 1950s.

At that time Bill Veeck, the controversial owner of the St. Louis Browns (of the American League), elected to compensate for the continual losing records of his club by attempting to lure fans to home games with some rather bizarre gimmicks.

One of the most memorable occurred on August 19, 1951.

With the Browns trailing the Detroit Tigers late in the second game of a doubleheader, Veeck called for a pinch hitter. That was no surprise. What followed was.

To the batter's box strode a 3-foot 7, 65-pound dwarf dressed in an official uniform, with his jersey displaying the number 1/8 on its back.

As the hitter—named Edward Carl Gaedel—stepped to the plate with his bat raised, Tigers manager Red Rolfe protested with gusto. Veeck, awaiting such a reaction, came out of the visitors' dugout carrying a copy of a legitimate contract. Home plate umpire Ed Hurley deemed everything to be in order after 15 minutes of spirited debate and allowed Gaedel to continue.

The diminutive hitter crouched at the plate, leaving a "strike zone" of barely over one inch.

As might be expected, Detroit pitcher Bob Cain walked Gaedel on four straight pitches.

St. Louis immediately replaced Gaedel with pinch runner Jim Delsing.

Within a span of less than one week, "for the sake of Major League Baseball," all major-league owners agreed that all players would be subject to acceptance by the commissioner.

In late 1961, following a night of heavy drinking at a local bowling alley, Gaedel was found dead in his bed by his mother. He was covered with bruises. The official medical report listed the cause of death as a heart attack.

The only former major-league player to attend his funeral was Detroit pitcher Bob Cain.

# WHY IS IT DIFFICULT FOR EVEN THE MOST LOYAL FAN TO DISTINGUISH EXACTLY WHICH PLAYERS ARE ON THE FIELD ON APRIL 15?

On one day each year, Major League Baseball honors one of its all-time "greats" by requiring every player, manager, and coach of both the visiting and home teams to wear the uniform number 42.

That was the number worn by the legendary Jack Roosevelt Robinson, the first African American to play in the majors when he inked a contract with the old Brooklyn Dodgers.

Robinson (better known as "Jackie") is heralded each year by all of big-league baseball on the anniversary of his entrance into the game: April 15, 1947. Jackie Robinson Day has been celebrated since 2004.

# WHY WERE NUMBERS MOVED TO THE BACKS OF UNIFORMS WORN BY BIG-LEAGUE PLAYERS?

In today's modern baseball parks, it's customary for fans to survey the backs of uniforms to identify their favorite players. But this custom wasn't always in place.

The first team to wear individually assigned numbers on its uniforms was the Cleveland Indians franchise on June 26, 1916.

The initial addition to the uniform came with little fanfare. First, the numbers appeared only on the sleeves of the uniforms, which did not draw as much attention as modern identifications do. While the relatively smaller size limited the view of the fans in the stands, some skeptics claimed that it compelled more of the paying customers to purchase scorecards, thus adding a few more dollars to the ballpark profits.

The practice was dubbed a gimmick by most of the media and discontinued after only a few weeks.

LOU GEHRIG'S NUMBER IS IMMORTALIZED IN THE
BASEBALL HALL OF FAME.

The first squad to create uniform numbers as we know them today—on the backs of jerseys—was the Yankees organization in the Bronx. In 1929 the Yankees identified the players by their spot in the batting order. Thus, Babe Ruth was given number 3, Lou Gehrig number 4, Bob Meusel number 5, and so on.

# WHY IS SOMEONE SELECTED TO TOSS OUT THE FIRST PITCH OF A MAJOR LEAGUE BASEBALL GAME?

No big-league baseball game today would begin, it seems, without observing the tradition of inviting someone (often a local celebrity) to stand on or near the pitcher's mound and throw what is normally called the "opening pitch" of the game.

This practice began as a result of an impromptu decision by the home-plate umpire prior to a game in 1910.

That game, scheduled between the hometown Washington Senators and the Philadelphia Athletics on April 14, sparked two happenings that are currently a regular part of every contest. (The second will be discussed in the next entry.)

The first took place even before the umpire-in-chief made the initial call of "Play ball!"

With invited dignitaries (including US president William Howard Taft) standing near the mound, umpire Billy Williams was tossed the official game ball. On a whim, Williams invited

PRESIDENT FRANKLIN ROOSEVELT THROWING OUT THE FIRST PITCH TO INAUGURATE THE 1936 SEASON.

the president to step up to the mound and throw the ball to the Washington catcher to signal the start of the game. President Taft, based on local reports of the time, said he was "delighted" by the honor.

Thus began another regular baseball "happening."

"IT AIN'T OVER 'TIL IT'S OVER."

YOGI BERRA

# WHY ARE FANS INVITED TO STAND PRIOR TO THE HOME HALF OF THE SEVENTH INNING?

Another familiar tradition throughout the country is one in which all visitors are invited to stand and stretch their legs in the seventh inning.

The ritual began as a result of a rather unexpected happening at the 1910 game mentioned in the previous entry, between the Senators and the Athletics.

It also involved the same president of the United States.

By the seventh inning of the contest, the 6-foot-2 Taft found it increasingly uncomfortable to sit in a wooden seat not designed for a 340-pound chief executive. So, unannounced, President Taft elected to take a quick stretch.

Thinking that the president was preparing to leave Griffith Stadium, most of the crowd stood as a symbol of respect. When the president sat back down in his chair, the fans realized their mistake and returned to their seats.

'16 - *Pres. Taft and party at base-ball game - Wash. D.C. - Copyright by B.M. Clinedinst Washington - D.C.*

*June 9 - 1910*

**FORMER PRESIDENT WILLIAM HOWARD TAFT AT A BASEBALL GAME IN 1918.**

The few seconds of stretch caused most of the people to appreciate the moment of relief—an observance reported in the next day's newspaper.

To this day, a respite from the discomfort of sitting in hard wooden seats for several hours is welcomed by even the most ardent fan.

As popular as this event is, and as much as it has become an accepted part of our game, it may surprise many of us that it began from an error in perception by a fan base more than 100 years ago.

# WHY ARE INTENTIONAL WALKS NOW GRANTED BEFORE A PITCH IS DELIVERED?

Prior to the 2017 season, a pitcher who wished to bypass a particular batter had to serve four pitches high and wide in order to issue a walk. It was his way of saying that he'd rather take his chances on the next opponent, typically a less accomplished batter.

The strategy is understandable and worked for many years—until 2017, when Major League Baseball ruled that, in order to save a few seconds of time that contributed to the growing length of games, all the pitcher has to do is to give a visual sign for the batter to move to first base.

How much time is saved through this change in rules is as yet unknown, but the figure might have to be left to statisticians who delight in calculating things like this.

# WHY DO TEAMS IN BOTH LEAGUES BEGIN EACH SEASON AT SPRING TRAINING CAMPS?

In the early days of Major League Baseball, all clubs started the season with what we know as Opening Day.

That all changed shortly before the start of the 20th century.

In 1886, President Albert Spalding of the old Chicago White Stockings (now the Chicago Cubs) decided that his players might gain a decisive advantage over opposing clubs were they to start practicing basic skills of pitching, fielding and hitting before facing those clubs.

He knew that none of his players would appreciate the thought of tossing a baseball in the winter cold of Chicago, so he moved his entire team to the more pleasant climate of the Baseball Grounds in Hot Springs, Arkansas. The exact amount of time they spent in Hot Springs is debatable.

White Stockings manager Cap Anson rationalized that Hot Springs, with its warm spring weather and mountains for

THE 1912 BROOKLYN DODGERS AT SPRING TRAINING IN HOT SPRINGS, ARKANSAS.

hiking, was an ideal setting to "boil out the alcoholic microbes in the hard-living players that were built up during the winter."

Spalding's theory must have worked. The White Stockings, who had finished with a winning record (87–25) and a first-place finish the previous season, gave their fans an encore performance with an equally impressive 90–34 record and an overpowering first-place finish.

It did not take the rest of the league long to conclude that spring training could also be of value to their clubs. Over the next few years, every big-league team followed suit.

# WHY DID THE 1895 PITTSBURGH PIRATES EMPLOY AN UNORTHODOX VERSION OF THE HIDDEN BALL TRICK?

Sometimes players and team managers go beyond all expectations to win ball games. The 1895 Pittsburgh Pirates were no exception to that truth.

A classic example took place during the managerial career of Cornelius McGillicuddy (better known as "Connie Mack").

The Pirates in '95 had what might be called a roller-coaster ride by having both long winning and long losing streaks that resulted in a 71–61 season and a seventh-place finish.

A noteworthy practice by the club at that time involved foul balls that landed on the roof of the stands that covered the fans seated inside Exposition Park.

A rumor circulating through the streets of Pittsburgh was that the night before a home game, someone inside the front office had the responsibility to place baseballs for the next day's game into a freezer with the belief that this would "freeze the life out of the balls."

In those days, umpires reused foul balls hit into the stands. When a player from the opposing team fouled a pitch onto the roof of the stadium, a young boy stationed there to retrieve foul balls would toss back one of the frozen balls. Its density would, according to the so-called experts of that time, prevent hitters from getting substantial distance out of a solid hit.

Although he did whatever he could to win baseball games, this was one story that Manager Mack neither acknowledged nor denied.

"IF IT WASN'T FOR BASEBALL,
I'D BE IN EITHER THE PENITENTIARY
OR THE CEMETERY."
**BABE RUTH**

# WHY ARE IDENTICAL BASEBALLS USED AT EACH VENUE IN THE MAJOR LEAGUES?

Another rumor floating around the country was that certain clubs used different baseballs in order to gain an advantage over the visiting opponents.

Let's say that one team had a lineup that consisted of an abundance of heavy hitters. That squad would benefit from using a lightweight ball that would be easier to smack over the outside fence. Another team consisting primarily of singles hitters would prefer to use a relatively heavy ball that would be more likely to stay inside the park.

In order to avoid the confusion (not to mention potential legal consequences) caused by questionable practices (such as the Pittsburgh Pirates' infamous hidden ball trick in the late 1800s), modern-day baseball ensures that no team will have an advantage over another through the use of custom baseballs.

As a result, every baseball used in every big-league stadium has uniform dimensions: circumference, nine inches; weight, five ounces; 108 hand-sewn red double stiches.

"A BALLPLAYER SPENDS A GOOD PIECE
OF HIS LIFE GRIPPING A BASEBALL,
AND IN THE END IT TURNS OUT THAT
IT WAS THE OTHER WAY AROUND
ALL THE TIME."
JIM BOUTON

# WHY DO THE STITCHES ON EACH BASEBALL HAVE THE SAME RED COLORING?

During the embryonic stages of baseball, not only did the sizes and weights of baseballs vary with locations, but so did the color of the stitching. As the game matured and the velocity of pitches increased, Major League Baseball demanded that each of its locations use balls with identical red thread.

The reason was pragmatic. To the hitter, a spinning ball with red thread is easier to see than a ball with stitching of any other color.

It, therefore, allows the batter a few fractions of a second to get out of the way if he determines that he might be struck by a 100-mph erratic fastball.

# WHY WERE PROFESSIONAL BASEBALL GAMES SOMETIMES PROHIBITED BY LAW TO GO THE FULL NINE INNINGS?

As sophisticated as we would like to think we have become in our lives, sometimes we forget how social mores have changed over the years.

Consider the era in American history when the majority of our nation was subject to rules for proper behavior in polite society. Unfortunately, acceptable deportment was identified not so much by laws adopted by the government. Of greater influence were what became known as "blue laws"—so named because they were first written on blue paper.

These laws, first reported as being observed in America as early as the 1620s, seldom appeared in any formal document such as the United States Constitution. Regardless, the consequences of disobedience could be devastating. Every citizen was to obey these puritanical practices, especially on the day of the week set aside for honoring the Lord.

These laws regulated activities regarding alcohol and tobacco sales, automotive sales, work hours, recreational activities, and a host of other "worldly affairs."

While blue laws were observed throughout the country, each state practiced its own specific litany of "shalts" and "shalt nots."

Forbidden practices included anything that resembled fun or recreation. That included playing or watching a baseball game.

In states that housed Major League Baseball teams, this presented a problem.

Both the Phillies of Philadelphia and their cross-state rivals, the Pirates of Pittsburgh, worked out an agreement with state authorities that no inning would start after 7:00 p.m. That would allow citizens enough time to watch baseball and still get to vespers—a specific evening worship of the liturgical churches.

Alas, along came the practice of playing Sunday double-headers. Quite often these games lasted past the 7:00 p.m. time limit. If any club disobeyed the law, it would be subject to a substantial fine.

Perhaps it was the result of cooler heads prevailing or just the pressure of big-league baseball, but throughout the nation all restrictions on the time and place for engaging in America's Pastime are now history.

# WHY ARE THE LOS ANGELES DODGERS IDENTIFIED BY SUCH A STRANGE TEAM NAME?

Like so many Major League Baseball teams that have changed locations for various reasons, the Dodgers kept their original name.

Walter O'Malley had worked hard to establish a solid reputation as co-owner of the Brooklyn Dodgers and as an entrepreneur and a pioneer in a variety of causes, including the signing of the first ever African American to a big-league franchise. As much as he loved the team and the people of Brooklyn, dwindling attendance at games plus the economics of the neighborhood forced him to consider the possibility of a move in 1957.

The question was: to where?

After careful consideration, the decision was Los Angeles, California.

What would he call the new team? The answer was easy. The name "Dodgers" had to remain with the franchise.

A CROWD OUTSIDE OF EBBETS FIELD IN BROOKLYN DURING THE 1920 WORLD SERIES.

But why such an unusual name in the first place?

Traversing Brooklyn in the late 19th century was akin to running a gauntlet. Coming at you at a relatively high rate of speed were electric trolley cars that compelled pedestrians to stay alert, at times even to jump out of the way in order to keep body and soul together.

Those who braved the unique challenge of walking in the borough were dubbed "trolley dodgers." Sportswriters soon adopted the name for the local baseball club, and it was shortened to just "Dodgers" in the 1930s. By that point Brooklyn natives considered a trip to Ebbets Field a walk in the park, but outsiders still thought it a challenge.

The team name—the "Dodgers"—stuck. All the way from Brooklyn to Los Angeles.

# WHY ARE THERE TWO DAYS DURING THE SEASON WHEN NO CLUB IN THE AMERICAN OR NATIONAL LEAGUE IS SCHEDULED TO PLAY A GAME?

Professional baseball teams squeeze in as many games as possible during the season in order to bring in as much revenue as possible to meet the increasing demands of high salaries. Nevertheless, there are two days during which every club is willing to leave the slate clean.

Those days would be the day before and the day after the All-Star Game.

The reason for this practice is logical. The day before the gathering, those talented athletes selected to appear in the contest need time to travel from their home cities to the scheduled city for the celebrated game. Likewise, the day following the game gives players adequate time to return home.

# WHY WAS A NINETEENTH-CENTURY UMPIRE DISCHARGED FROM MAJOR LEAGUE BASEBALL?

It's a testimony to the integrity of those who have been selected to umpire the bases and call balls and strikes for big-league baseball that only one person has ever been banned from the sport because of misbehavior. And it happened way back in 1882.

His name was Dick Higham.

It wasn't Higham's lack of skills that led to his demise as an arbiter. Instead, it was his "sideline occupation" that caused a problem.

Mr. Higham loved to gamble—and he brought that love to the very games he umpired, placing bets on certain teams and then ensuring their success. He judged several close calls to rule in favor of the team on which he had placed a wager shortly before the game started.

In addition, Higham was probably not the brightest of those bent on engaging in unethical practices. The disgraced umpire's behavior behind the scenes became known to every baseball fan when a private detective uncovered correspondence about the scheme between Higham and his gaming partner.

"I'VE NEVER QUESTIONED THE INTEGRITY OF AN UMPIRE. THEIR EYESIGHT, YES."

LEO DUROCHER

# WHY IS THE ACRONYM WHIP NOW USED TO INDICATE THE EFFECTIVENESS OF A PITCHER?

WHIP is a rather recent addition to the methodology of evaluating and comparing pitchers. It has been in use since 1979.

The letters stand for "Walks plus Hits per Innings Pitched."

WHIP is one sophisticated tool employed in this era of sabermetric player analysis. It's a way of measuring the efficacy of a pitcher beyond the familiar earned run average.

As of 2019, the best single-season WHIP record belongs to Pedro Martinez of the Boston Red Sox for the 2000 season.

# WHY IS A BALK AN ILLEGAL PITCH IN BASEBALL?

A balk is an illegal maneuver by a pitcher meant to intentionally deceive a batter into thinking that a pitch is on its way when it's not. There are many ways to balk, including the pitcher feinting or halting a pitch to the plate or beginning a pitch then throwing to a base while on the rubber. The balk rule exists to prevent these deceptions. The penalty for a balk is all base runners (not including the batter) advance one base.

# WHY HAVE CERTAIN STAR PLAYERS NOT BEEN CONSIDERED FOR SELECTION TO THE HALL OF FAME?

One of the most common of all baseball arguments among fans occurs during the selection of new inductees to the Hall of Fame—especially when a favorite player is not selected. That's particularly the case when it involves a player who had demonstrated a superb amount of talent.

Two examples come to mind.

The first is "Shoeless" Joe Jackson, who was accused of fixing the infamous 1919 World Series between his Chicago White Sox and the Cincinnati Reds. Baseball commissioner Kenesaw Mountain Landis ruled that Jackson and seven of his teammates took bribes to lose the World Series that year.

The second is Pete Rose, who holds the all-time record for hits in the big leagues (4,256) plus a multitude of other records. Rose was found guilty in 1989 of gambling on baseball games while he was serving as manager of the Cincinnati Reds.

Both Jackson and Rose are on the "ineligible" list for the Hall of Fame. It seems that player stats cannot overcome personal failings. More detailed information on both of these talented players appears elsewhere in this book.

"A BASEBALL SWING IS A VERY FINELY TUNED INSTRUMENT. IT IS REPETITION, AND MORE REPETITION, THEN A LITTLE MORE AFTER THAT."

**REGGIE JACKSON**

# WHY DO MOST EXPERTS CONSIDER BABE RUTH THE GREATEST BASEBALL PLAYER WHO EVER LIVED?

Want to create a topic for a spirited discussion among avid baseball fans? Ask any assembled group, "Who was the greatest player of all time?"

Depending on the generation represented, you'll get a variety of responses.

However, after all the dust has settled and all the alcoholic beverages have been consumed, the facts clearly identify one player. His name was George Herman "Babe" Ruth.

Of course, an avalanche of skeptics might chime in with statistics designed to support other candidates, but respected journalist Blake Apgar, in a recent edition of the *Las Vegas Review-Journal*, lists a thumbnail sketch of the Babe's accomplishments that seems unassailable. The "Sultan of Swat" simply leaves all other candidates behind.

The most obvious distinction is that Babe Ruth not only was one of the greatest sluggers of all time, but also ranks

BABE RUTH, PERHAPS THE GREATEST BASEBALL PLAYER OF ALL TIME.

among the most outstanding hurlers who ever stepped onto the mound.

Take an objective look at his phenomenal accomplishments as he played for the Boston Red Sox (1914–1919), the New York Yankees (1920–1934), and the Boston Braves (1935). Apgar lists some eye-popping figures:

Home runs: 714 (3rd in MLB history)

Batting average: .342 (10th in MLB history)

Hits: 2,873

Runs batted in: 2,213 (2nd in MLB history)

Slugging percentage: .690 (1st in MLB history)

On-base percentage: .474 (2nd in MLB history)

Pitching record: 94–46

ERA: 2.28

**"I KNOW, BUT I HAD A BETTER YEAR THAN HOOVER."**

BABE RUTH, REPLYING TO A REPORTER WHO OBJECTED THAT THE SALARY RUTH WAS DEMANDING ($80,000) WAS MORE THAN THAT OF PRESIDENT HERBERT HOOVER ($75,000)

# WHY ARE BABE RUTH'S OFFICIAL RECORDS OF 714 HOME RUNS AND 2,213 RBIS ACTUALLY UNDERSTATEMENTS OF HIS BRILLIANT LEGACY?

While Ruth's career is something any big-leaguer would be proud to claim, his numbers would be even greater were the Bambino playing under the current rules of measuring statistics.

When Ruth was sending baseballs over the wall, with runners on base, to win games in the last inning, the official scorers counted only the tying and winning runs that crossed the plate. The batter was credited with hitting only a single, double, or triple; the winning run broke the tie and the game was considered over at that point.

Based upon the records made available from that era, the Babe actually hit at least three more homers than first believed.

The rule was changed in 1920 to allow all runs scored by a last-minute four-bagger.

# WHY WAS BABE RUTH GIVEN SUCH A STRANGE NICKNAME?

It might appear odd that a man of such impressive stature (6-foot-2, 215 pounds) would be tagged with a nickname more appropriate for an infant. Yet that's precisely why it happened.

Plenty of stories have circulated throughout the years as to why this odd nickname was bestowed on George Herman Ruth Jr. The correct story, according to most historians, resulted from events when he was 19 years old, though the name was suggested well before that.

Ruth was an unpredictable youngster who needed strong adult supervision to keep him on the straight and narrow. That leadership came in the person of a Roman Catholic monk who was on the faculty of St. Mary's Industrial School in Baltimore.

His name was Brother Matthias.

The monk took a liking to Ruth when the youngster first came to the school, not yet a teenager. He saw in Ruth the raw talent for stardom in baseball.

Over the next few years, Brother Matthias taught Ruth the fundamentals of hitting, fielding, and pitching. Matthias called his good friend Jack Dunn, owner of the Baltimore Orioles, to take a look at the young prospect.

It took less than an hour for Dunn to see that this boy was a diamond in the rough. Since George was not yet of legal age, Mr. Dunn became his legal guardian to complete the contract.

When the youngster first arrived at the Orioles' training camp, he was labeled as "Jack's newest babe."

The name stuck.

Later that year, Ruth was sold to the Red Sox, and the nickname followed him.

During his first trip to the mound in an exhibition game, he kept striking out batters for the Red Sox. One of his teammates remarked, "Look at him mow down those batters. And he still looks like a little baby while doing it."

That was the only endorsement the young man needed. George Herman Ruth thereafter was known as "Babe."

# WHY DID BABE RUTH LEAVE A NO-HIT GAME WITHOUT RETIRING A SINGLE BATTER?

Babe Ruth started a game on June 23, 1917, against the Washington Senators by walking the leadoff hitter, Ray Morgan.

Ruth thought his last pitch had actually caught the outside corner, but home plate umpire Brick Owens had a different opinion and shouted out, "Ball four."

The Red Sox pitcher (a fierce competitor, indeed) rushed from the mound to protest the call. Umpire Owens held his ground. When Ruth's words became too intense, the umpire tossed him out of the game.

According to some reports, Ruth even took a swing at the arbiter that struck him on the back of his neck.

Relief pitcher Ernie Shore replaced Ruth and watched Morgan attempt to steal second, but he was unsuccessful.

Then, to the delight of his teammates, Shore proceeded to dispose of the next 26 batters in order.

The verdict: Ernie Shore was credited with a no-hitter. Babe Ruth got zilch.

"PEOPLE ASK ME WHAT I DO IN WINTER WHEN THERE'S NO BASEBALL. I'LL TELL YOU WHAT I DO. I STARE OUT THE WINDOW AND WAIT FOR SPRING."

ROGERS HORNSBY

# WHY DID DON LARSEN COME CLOSE TO NOT PITCHING THE GREATEST GAME IN THE HISTORY OF THE WORLD SERIES?

The game of baseball is akin to real life with the volume turned up. If one game is deemed important, fans and sportscasters may discuss and analyze that contest for generations.

Moreover, if something happens during that contest that is so spectacular that it must be labeled as absolutely "perfect," that, in and of itself, needs no further description.

Only one game ever played in the history of Major League Baseball fits that description.

It happened on October 8, 1956.

That was the date of the fifth game of the World Series between the archrival Brooklyn Dodgers and New York Yankees.

The scheduled mound opponents that afternoon were two veteran hurlers: Sal Maglie (119–62 lifetime record) for Brooklyn and Don Larsen (81–91 lifetime record) for the Yankees.

It had all the earmarks of a classic matchup. Except for one thing: The Yankees' Larsen, who was never told that he was going to pitch that day, had spent the previous evening at a local bar. In fact, he did not arrive to the stadium until just about an hour prior to game time. Only then did he discover that he was going to pitch—hangover and all.

To the delight of the 64,519 fans packed into Yankee Stadium that afternoon, Larsen retired the Dodgers in order in the top half of the first. Maglie equaled that feat. That set the stage for everyone in the stands and the thousands who were watching on television. This was going to be a pitchers' duel.

The Yankees got just five hits that afternoon, one of which was a towering shot into the stands by the slugging Mickey Mantle. But this was enough to keep the Dodgers in check. Larsen did not allow anyone to score. In fact, he did not allow any Dodger to reach base.

By the ninth inning, the Yankees were ahead 2–0. The only thing going through the mind of every fan viewing the action was whether Don Larsen could pull off a modern miracle by tossing a no-hit, no run perfect game.

Three batters later, when pinch-hitter Dale Mitchell came to the plate, Larsen calmly retired him on a firmly called "Strike three!" Home plate umpire Babe Pinelli made the call, though the pitch appeared to be wide of the plate.

THE HARTFORD COURANT • Sunday, Oct. 7, 1956

## With Malice Toward None
By BILL LEE — Sports Editor

# Big Don Larsen Hurls Perfect Game

## Don Larsen Is Known For Hitting

## Yankees Triumph 2-0 On Greatest Pitching In Baseball's History

SAYS SAL-TO DON, 'IT WAS PERFECT!'

YANKEE OWNERS HAPPY WITH LARSEN'S FEAT

## Ernie Shore Adds Praise For Larsen

WINSTON-SALEM, N. C., Oct. 6

SCHALLEY SALVAGES SOUVENIR

## Larsen In Daze, Doesn't Believe It; Credits Prayers, Mates For Feat
By DON LARSEN

Official Box Score

## List Of Baseball's Perfect Games

Sports on the Air

THE *HARTFORD COURANT* HEADLINE THE DAY AFTER DON LARSEN'S PERFECT GAME.

The hometown fans and everyone else who viewed the game knew they had witnessed a classic. And, in spite of suffering through that gnawing hangover from the night before, Don Larsen probably remembered each one of the 97 pitches he threw that glorious afternoon in 1956.

"BASEBALL IS A RED-BLOODED SPORT FOR RED-BLOODED MEN. IT'S NO PINK TEA, AND MOLLYCODDLES HAD BETTER STAY OUT. IT'S A STRUGGLE FOR SUPREMACY, A SURVIVAL OF THE FITTEST."

TY COBB

# WHY WAS ONE HITTER, WITH ONE SWING, SAID TO TURN THE ENTIRE BASEBALL WORLD UPSIDE DOWN BY DOING THE "IMPOSSIBLE"?

Baseball is filled to overflowing with heroic tales that defy logic.

This may be the only way to describe what happened on October 15, 1988, when a former football star from Michigan State University gave an unforgettable memory to every baseball fan who refused to allow an impossible scene to be confined to a comic book or to the imagination of a fiction writer.

Some 55,983 fans attended the opening game of the '88 World Series inside Los Angeles's Dodger Stadium, and millions of enthusiasts followed the action via radio and television. Even the most optimistic were stunned beyond belief.

The American League Champion As had won an impressive 104 games during the regular season with standout performances from sluggers Jose Canseco and Mark McGwire. The Dodgers, too, had star power, including hard-hitting Kirk Gibson and pitching sensation Orel Hershiser. The only difference was that Gibson was unavailable. In fact, he could barely walk. He was nursing an injured right knee and a compromised hamstring in his left leg.

While the rest of his teammates were being introduced to the overflow crowd, the League's Most Valuable Player, Gibson, was in the trainer's room receiving a painful cortisone shot.

The As established an early 4–2 lead when Canseco blasted a grand-slam home run in the second inning.

The Dodgers were able to get one more run by the bottom half of the ninth.

Things looked grim for the home team when the As sent to the mound their greatest relief pitcher, Dennis Eckersley– MVP of the Junior Circuit.

Eckersley retired the first two Dodgers as some of the Dodger fans started to head for the exits. Then Eckersley, who had walked only two batters the entire year, sent some of those fans back to their seats when he issued pinch hitter Mike Davis a free pass.

That set the stage. Announcer Vin Scully noted that this would be the ideal time to call Kirk Gibson to the plate. But Scully was quick to set aside all hope for that drama, explaining that Gibson was "not even in uniform."

KIRK GIBSON CELEBRATES HIS GAME-WINNING HOME RUN IN THE 1988 WORLD SERIES.

Not often was Vin Scully shown to be wrong during his illustrious career, but to his astonishment, suddenly emerging from the Dodger dugout appeared a hobbling Kirk Gibson.

"Manager Tommy Lasorda is looking for lightning in a bottle," exclaimed Scully.

The fans erupted with gusto.

Gibson was obviously in pain as he fouled off two pitches from Eckersley. The savvy relief hurler tried to get Gibson to take a third called strike, but home-plate umpire Doug Harvey called all three pitches too far outside.

Then Eckersley tried to sneak a slider past Gibson. But the hobbling Dodger leaned on his left foot and, with only one hand, swung and smacked the ball. It sailed off toward deep right field.

The As could only stand in awe and watch the ball as it sailed above the wall.

Gibson also watched the ball disappear out of sight before raising both arms over his head in justifiable celebration.

The fans screamed as loudly as ever in Dodger history.

In one instant, Dodger broadcasting legend Scully coined a classic expression that crystalized what everyone understood to be true: "In the year of the improbable, the impossible has happened."

Anyone who was there will truly remember this once-in-a-lifetime moment forever. As will the millions of fans who were watching around the world.

# WHY DID ONE "BEAN BALL" CHANGE THE CAREER OF A YOUNG CENTER FIELDER?

If you lived in New York City during the early 1950s, you were surrounded by some rich baseball traditions. There were the New York Yankees, the New York Giants, and the Brooklyn Dodgers.

The neighborhood in which you were raised determined which of these three teams became your team. And that affiliation was with you for the rest of your life.

That was true for a teenager named Mario, the son of two immigrants from Salerno, Italy, who set for him another conviction: to study hard at school in order to be the best in whatever career he chose.

Mario heeded their urging—particularly his father's—to get good grades. But young Mario also was lured into following the game of baseball.

Not only did he follow the game. He excelled at it.

His favorite position was center field. There he could take advantage of his remarkable speed and his talent for hitting a long ball.

During the summer months, when he was a young teen, he tried out for a traveling team from his Queens neighborhood. He not only made the squad, but he became the starting center fielder.

One of the earliest trips for the youngster was to Fort Monmouth, New Jersey, to play a game against some veterans. In the crowd, watching the action on the field, happened to be Ed McCarrick, the chief scout from the Pittsburgh Pirates. He was captivated by the obvious talent of the speedy center fielder. In fact, immediately following the game, McCarrick offered Mario a contract and a signing bonus of $2,000.

Mario was eager to break the news to his father. Because he was still in high school, he needed his father to sign the contract. He knew that would be no problem.

Mario was wrong.

"Absolutely not," responded his father. "You are going to finish your high school education."

"But, Pop . . . I . . ."

"I have spoken," said his father in a tone that Mario knew meant the discussion was over.

McCarrick wrote a letter to Mario's father in which he promised that his son would not have to play ball for the Pirates' farm team until he completed school. Mario promised that he would not touch a baseball until after he graduated. On the basis of that compromise, the father signed the contract.

GOVERNOR MARIO CUOMO OF NEW YORK TAKES A FEW SWINGS BEFORE A GAME IN 1984.

Mario's first trip in the minor leagues was to Brunswick, Georgia, where he batted .252 and showed that he could hit a long ball and cover center field with relative ease.

Suddenly, Mario's dreams of making it to the majors were shattered. Late in the season, in a game in which he had gotten two hits, Mario had to duck out of the way of a high, inside fastball.

He didn't duck quickly enough. The ball hit Mario in the head, sending him to the hospital with a severe concussion.

During a long month recovering, he thought about his future in baseball. As much as he loved the sport, he knew he would never become another Joe DiMaggio.

Alone in that hospital bed, he received an academic scholarship offer from St. John's University in Queens. He made the decision to accept the offer.

His passion for academics replaced his zeal for baseball, and he eventually realized he had made the right decision. Especially on November 2, 1982, when Mario M. Cuomo was elected to be the fifty-second governor of the State of New York.

# WHY DO UMPIRES USE HAND SIGNALS TO CALL BALLS AND STRIKES?

Using hand signals to call balls and strikes has been a tradition since the 1880s. It began when a member of the Washington Nationals requested that hand signals be used to benefit an outfielder who was deaf.

William "Dummy" Hoy had lost his hearing at the age of two as a result of spinal meningitis. (Nicknames were far less politically correct in his day than now.) Hoy was a fierce base runner who led the National League in steals his rookie year.

Because he could not hear the umpire call a ball and, while on base, had to wait for several seconds to see the reactions of the batter and catcher before attempting to steal a base, Hoy was at a disadvantage compared to any other runner.

Hoy convinced the home-plate umpire to raise his arm when he called a strike.

Since then, hand signals by umpires have been a regular part of the game.

# WHY ARE THE OUTFIELD WALLS OF CHICAGO'S WRIGLEY FIELD COVERED WITH IVY?

Fans of the Chicago Cubs will agree that no picture of the brick fencing designating the outer boundaries of Wrigley Field would be complete without including the unique covering of ivy.

The idea of ivy covering the brick façade of Wrigley goes back to 1937, when chewing gum magnate and team owner Philip Wrigley, who knew a thing or two about promotions and packaging, decided to create an "outdoor experience"

"THERE ARE ONLY TWO SEASONS: WINTER AND BASEBALL."

**BILL VEECK**

THE IVY-COVERED WALLS IN THE OUTFIELD AT WRIGLEY FIELD IN CHICAGO.

that fans would enjoy while cheering their team on the north side of Chicago.

Mr. Wrigley conveyed the idea to one of his young executives, Bill Veeck. Veeck, along with other club officials, thought that planting ivy at the base of the wall and allowing the foliage to grow upward, to the top of the wall, would create "a woodsy feel" that would invite fans to escape the grime of the city and to relax while watching their favorite team in action.

The plan has worked for more than 80 years.

# WHY DO FIELDERS USE DIFFERENT SHAPES AND SIZES OF BASEBALL GLOVES?

Until about 1870, baseball players wore absolutely no gloves when fielding their positions. One of the first to don a glove was Doug Allison, a catcher for the Cincinnati Red Stockings.

More and more players soon realized the advantage of protection for their bare hands (especially during the colder months of the year), even though most of the early gloves had the fingertips cut off. It wasn't until 1920 that a St. Louis pitcher wore a glove with webbing between the thumb and index finger that created a pocket for easier fielding. It's a basic design that remains standard to this day.

The official rules of baseball specify the size of gloves and the materials from which they can be made.

Certain "specialty" gloves have their own criteria for acceptance. A catcher's mitt, for example, has no fingers but a claw-like pocket that allows a player to snag errant pitches.

A first baseman may use a larger mitt than other infielders, one that allows him to scoop balls thrown into the dirt. The first to use such a glove was Hall of Famer Hank Greenberg, slugging icon of the Detroit Tigers.

Infielders wear gloves that are noticeably smaller and make it easier for the fielder to snatch a ground ball and throw a runner out at first.

Pitchers normally use gloves with closed webbings to conceal the ball from the eyes of the batter, who might be able to determine what pitch is coming by the way the pitcher grips the ball.

Outfielders have more flexibility, but most use gloves with deep pockets that allow them to make spectacular diving catches.

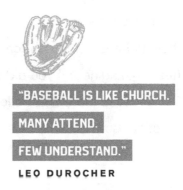

"BASEBALL IS LIKE CHURCH.

MANY ATTEND.

FEW UNDERSTAND."

LEO DUROCHER

# WHY DID OUTFIELDERS PRIOR TO THE MID-1950S THROW DOWN THEIR GLOVES AT THE CONCLUSION OF EACH INNING?

For many years it appeared as though outfielders abandoned their gloves at the end of each inning. They tossed them down, letting the gloves remain where they landed, and did not retrieve them until they returned to their defensive positions.

Why did both the National and American Leagues follow this strange ritual?

Some said it was bad luck to take your glove with you when you returned to the dugout. Most players admitted that they had absolutely no idea whether there was some benefit (real or imagined) if you did this.

Because there was no logical purpose to maintaining the practice, both leagues disbanded the ritual in 1954.

# WHY DID MOST SUPERSTARS OF DAYS GONE BY PLAY THEIR ENTIRE CAREERS WITH JUST ONE TEAM?

Unlike the most talented players who wear Major League Baseball uniforms today, prior to the mid-1970s players were bound by portion of their contracts called the reserve clause, which was introduced to big-league ball in 1879. It said that the player had to stay with a particular team until that team elected to sell him or trade him to another team. In short, it was the team that had complete control over where the player would compete in any given year.

All came to a screeching halt in 1975 when an arbitrator named Peter Seitz nullified the reserve clause. He sided with two players—Andy Messersmith and David McNally—who felt that they were deprived of the basic right given to every American to work at any legal endeavor for any company (or team) that he so chooses.

Had free agency (as it was dubbed by the press) been the rule prior to 1975, there's an excellent chance that Hall of

Famers such as Stan Musial, Ted Williams, Carl Yastrzemski, Al Kaline, Jim Palmer, Bob Gibson, Roberto Clemente, and Willie Stargell would have played for multiple teams.

"NO MATTER HOW GOOD YOU ARE, YOU'RE GOING TO LOSE ONE-THIRD OF YOUR GAMES. NO MATTER HOW BAD YOU ARE, YOU'RE GOING TO WIN ONE-THIRD OF YOUR GAMES. IT'S THE OTHER THIRD THAT MAKES THE DIFFERENCE."

**TOMMY LASORDA**

# WHY ARE CURRENT BASEBALL FRANCHISES INCREASING IN VALUE AT ALARMING RATES?

Few financial investments have been as profitable for investors as ownership of a Major League Baseball team. There are several reasons for this fact.

1) Lucrative contracts generated between television networks and teams. Deals with FOX, TBS, and ESPN, for example, have generated about $1.5 billion a year and will continue to do so through 2021.

2) In line with this, local television contracts with regional sports networks add, according to some analysts, hundreds of millions of dollars to the balance sheets of teams serving highly populated areas of the country.

3) Fans throughout the nation have subscribed to regional coverage of their favorite teams.

4) Major League Baseball has enjoyed a relative peace in negotiations since 1994, the last year there was a strike or lockout.

5) Revenue sharing allows smaller markets to actually profit, because teams in higher-populated areas must "donate" some of their additional income to those smaller markets.

"AS I GREW UP, I KNEW THAT AS A BUILDING, [FENWAY PARK] WAS ON THE LEVEL OF MOUNT OLYMPUS, THE PYRAMID AT GIZA, THE NATION'S CAPITOL, THE CZAR'S WINTER PALACE, AND THE LOUVRE— EXCEPT, OF COURSE, THAT IT'S BETTER THAN ALL THOSE INCONSEQUENTIAL PLACES."

**BART GIAMATTI**

# WHY IS THE 1960 WORLD SERIES A TRUE TESTIMONIAL TO YOGI BERRA'S ADAGE "IT AIN'T OVER 'TIL IT'S OVER"?

The year 1960 marked the beginning of remarkable changes in American history. A young, Roman Catholic US senator named John Fitzgerald Kennedy was elected president of the nation and the so-called establishment suddenly realized that the torch of leadership had passed to a new generation. It was the start of the "Age of Aquarius," which challenged heretofore accepted norms about the family, about blind obedience to the letter of the law, and even about faithfulness to the religion in which a person was raised.

Prior to 1960, Major League Baseball embraced its own sense of traditional standards. The reserve clause bound players inextricably to their teams unless they were traded or released. When a manager gave an order, he was obeyed without question. And, of course, the New York Yankees were expected to win the World Series. Some traditions were sacred.

The mighty New York Yankees had won the American League pennant by posting a 97–57 record. The team sported many headliners such as Mickey Mantle, Roger Maris, Yogi Berra, and other household names.

The rival Pittsburgh Pirates had an impressive 95–59 record, led by Vernon Law, Dick Groat, and perhaps the best fielding second baseman in all of baseball, Bill Mazeroski.

The World Series matchup produced several lopsided scores, in most of which the Yankees prevailed.

Pittsburgh won the first game 6–4 at the Steel City's Forbes Field. As if to say enough is enough, the Yankees rolled up their sleeves and won Games 2 and 3 by scores of 16–3 and 10–0.

Law and reliever Elroy Face combined to squeak out a 3–2 victory against the Yanks in Game 4. In spite of a home run clubbed by Roger Maris, the Bucs also won Game 5, a 5–2 victory.

Back in Pittsburgh for Game 6, Pirate fans sang their theme song: "The Bucs Are Going All the Way." But perhaps they hit a few sour notes, as the Yankees clobbered the Pirates 12–0.

That set the stage for what many fans still call the greatest ending in the history of baseball.

The early morning sun peeking over the horizon on October 13, 1960, brought out a colorful fall kaleidoscope of scarlet, lemon, and gold leaves still clinging to the trees in

Schenley Park just beyond the outfield walls of Forbes Field. It seemed as though some of nature's finery wanted to linger just to witness what was about to happen.

Were any fiction writer to have submitted to a publisher the script for the 1960 World Series, especially for Game 7, it probably would have been rejected as being unrealistic. But that's just one of the rewards of baseball: the predictable is not an ironclad guarantee.

Pirates manager Danny Murtaugh, in a gutsy move, benched his leading home-run hitter, first baseman Dick Stuart, in favor of the better fielding Rocky Nelson. Law was given the ball to start the game for Pittsburgh, while "Bullet Bob" Turley was the choice of Yankees manager Casey Stengel.

Law got off to a great start as the Pirates established a rather comfortable lead of 4–0. But Moose Skowron's homer in the fifth gave the Yankees their first tally. When Face replaced Law in the sixth, a single by Mickey Mantle made the score 4–2, and a towering home run by Yogi Berra gave New York a 5–4 lead.

A curtain of gloom fell upon the partisan crowd of 36,683.

The once beautiful sky seemed to grow darker when the Yankees increased their lead by two more runs in the top half of the eighth.

However, the Bucs were not through. Following a single by the Bucs in the eighth, Bill Virdon hit what looked like a sure double-play grounder to short. The ball hit a pebble on the surface of the field, took a wicked hop, and caught shortstop Tony Kubek in the Adam's apple. Kubek dropped to the ground. Both runners were ruled safe. A single from Groat made the score 7–5. Roberto Clemente beat out an infield hit to score Virdon and put the Pirates within one run.

Then Hal Smith, a reserve catcher who had hit only 11 home runs all year, etched his name into Pirates immortality when he smacked a 1–2 pitch over the left-center field wall, giving the Pirates a 9–7 lead.

The roar of the crowd may have registered a seven on the Richter Scale as broadcaster Chuck Thompson exclaimed, "Pittsburgh has just become an insane asylum. We have seen and shared in one of baseball's great moments."

The stage was now set for the most bizarre ending to a World Series.

In the top half of the ninth, the Yankees scored two runs highlighted by a back-to-first slide by baserunner Mickey Mantle, who beat by a whisker a swiping tag by first baseman Nelson.

The score was knotted at 9.

Leading off the bottom of the ninth, Mazeroski faced Yankee hurler Ralph Terry.

The giant Longines clock atop the left-field scoreboard showed the time as 3:36.

BILL MAZEROSKI'S BOTTOM-OF-THE-NINTH HOME RUN IN GAME 7 OF THE 1960
WORLD SERIES CAPPED WHAT THIS NEWSPAPER CALLED "THE MOST DRAMATIC
FINALE IN SERIES HISTORY."

On a 1–0 count, Mazeroski swung at a high fastball and it went high and deep to left field. Yogi Berra, playing left field that afternoon, ran toward the wall and stood helplessly as he watched the 400-foot blast disappear into the trees in Schenley Park. Berra fell to his knees, realizing that the ball and the World Series were out of his reach.

The 24-year-old Mazeroski ran, skipped, and hopped around the bases, waving his hat over his head. Some fans ran onto the field and followed him. The rest of the audience roared like a Bessemer converter at US Steel.

In the visitors' locker room, the Yankees sat in stoned silence. Berra summed up the feelings of his team: "It was the first time I saw Mickey Mantle cry."

"YOU CAN SHAKE A DOZEN GLOVE MEN OUT OF A TREE, BUT THE BAT SEPARATES THE MEN FROM THE BOYS."

**DALE LONG**

# WHY WAS THE NATIONAL BASEBALL HALL OF FAME AND MUSEUM ESTABLISHED IN COOPERSTOWN, NEW YORK?

One of the most familiar landmarks in America is located in a remote setting in northern New York. It draws people from every state in the Union not because it is the site of a great historic happening, as is Gettysburg, or because it contains some inspiring natural beauty, as does the Grand Canyon. In fact, the original reason for putting the Baseball Hall of Fame in Cooperstown was based on what most people consider an untruth.

The idea of establishing an attraction for tourists was generated in 1935 when members of the Clark Foundation in Cooperstown wanted to revive business and tourism following the Great Depression. They proclaimed with certainty that a former army officer—Abner Doubleday, a native of Cooperstown—had invented the game of baseball in 1839. The members lobbied politicians and other influential people

THE BASEBALL HALL OF FAME IN COOPERSTOWN, NEW YORK.

throughout the state to have a museum to the sport be built and set aside to promote baseball.

Their claims regarding Doubleday were disputed by many insiders; nonetheless, foundation members continued to promote the story and proceeded with plans to erect the museum.

As to who would be honored as nominees to the Hall, the founders asked the Baseball Writers' Association of America (BBWAA) to manage the selection process. Inductees had to receive 75 percent of the votes cast, which is still a criterion today.

The first members, selected in 1936, were Ty Cobb, Babe Ruth, Honus Wagner, Christy Mathewson, and Walter Johnson.

# WHY WERE COBB, RUTH, WAGNER, MATHEWSON, AND JOHNSON SELECTED AS THE INAUGURAL CLASS FOR THE HALL OF FAME?

The first members so honored are no surprise to any seasoned fan of baseball.

The first inductee, and the one who received the largest amount of votes of the 226 ballots cast, was Tyrus Raymond Cobb (222 votes). Quite possibly he'll be regarded as the greatest hitter of all time. This outstanding slugger won nine batting titles from 1907 to 1915.

Tying for second in votes (215) were George Herman "Babe" Ruth, who was an outstanding pitcher and record-making home-run hitter, and Honus Wagner, who won eight batting titles and collected more than 3,000 hits.

Christy Mathewson pitched more winning games than anyone else who had stood on the mound and received 205 votes.

THE INAUGURAL CLASS OF THE BASEBALL HALL OF FAME. LEFT TO RIGHT, TOP TO BOTTOM: CHRISTY MATHEWSON, BABE RUTH, TY COBB, HONUS WAGNER, AND WALTER JOHNSON.

Finally, Walter Johnson received 189 votes for the superb record for strikeouts he held at his retirement.

Four of these five were present at their official induction on June 12, 1939. Missing was Christy Mathewson, who had died in October 1925.

# WHY HAS A UNIVERSITY PROFESSOR BEEN CREATING MLB SCHEDULES SINCE 2005?

For 24 years, a husband-and-wife team scheduled MLB teams using both computer programs and old-fashioned pencil and paper. But in 2005, a new group bid for the scheduling contract and won with software that reduces semi-repeaters, avoids conflicts, and streamlines the process.

Dr. Michael Trick, a professor of operations research at Carnegie Mellon University in Pittsburgh, developed the system with associates at his company, Sports Scheduling Group. They arrange schedules for Major League Baseball teams as well as for umpires throughout the year.

According to Trick, making the baseball schedule is like no other task because "we have to worry about travel time and distances that make sense to all the teams. Also, teams like to be home for a week to ten days and on the road for a week or ten days."

In addition, Major League Baseball requires a double round-robin (a home-and-home series) among division opponents from the last week in August through the end of the regular season.

Complicating matters even further, there's the constant desire from every team to minimize travel due to the fatigue resulting from longer trips. Also, television networks want marquee matchups on key dates to maximize ratings. Other clubs want their teams home on specific dates to celebrate milestones in the histories of their franchises or mark the retirements of star players.

In order to keep the complaints that would normally be associated with such a complex arrangement to a minimum, Trick and his colleagues send a form to each club asking for specific dates they'd like to be home and for any additional items they might wish to include in the schedule for the upcoming season.

It's up to each club to determine the starting time for each of its 81 home games.

# WHY DID ONE MAJOR-LEAGUE PITCHER REGRET THE BEST GAME OF HIS CAREER?

Sometimes in baseball things are just not fair. Such was the case on September 9, 1965, at Dodger Stadium in Los Angeles.

It was a game between the visiting Chicago Cubs (who were going nowhere that year) and the first-place Dodgers.

The Cubbies had a few notables on their roster. Outfielder Billy Williams, for example, hit .315 that year and belted 34 round-trippers. Also, third baseman Ron Santo and first baseman Ernie Banks were constant threats at the plate. Los Angeles's major weapon was two-fold: pitchers Don Drysdale and, quite possibly the greatest southpaw in history, Sandy Koufax.

The starting pitchers that evening were Charles "Bob" Hendley, who entered the game with a seven-year record of 27–42, and Koufax, whose record was a stark contrast. The 6-foot-2 Brooklyn native set the standard against which every other hurler was compared. He would finish the year with 26 wins, 382 strikeouts, and 27 complete games thrown.

The game was considered to be such a mismatch that Las Vegas oddsmakers eliminated the game from the betting boards.

When the game started, to the surprise of absolutely nobody, Koufax retired the Cubs in the first inning. What was unexpected, however, was that Hendley matched him batter for batter. In fact, neither pitcher allowed a hit by the opposing team over the first four innings.

When Koufax retired the Cubs in the top half of the fifth, some in the stands whispered among themselves that Koufax might be on the brink of something special. Those fans were aware of an old superstition in baseball: once someone dares to mention that a pitcher is throwing a no-hitter, the next batter is sure to get a hit.

Lou Johnson walked to lead off the Dodgers' half of the fifth as Ron Fairly sacrificed him to second. With one out, manager Walter Alston ordered Johnson to steal third. The Cubs catcher fired a bullet to third, but his throw was off-target and sailed into left field. Johnson scored easily.

Dodgers 1, Cubs 0.

Hendley retired the next two batters.

Team announcers Vin Scully of the Dodgers and Harry Caray of the Cubs mentioned on air that they had not before seen two teams so dominated by pitching.

In the bottom of the seventh, with two outs, Johnson blooped a pop fly just inside the right-field line, just out of reach of Banks. It fell in short right field for a double. Fairly grounded out to end the inning.

The fans may have not mentioned that Koufax was throwing a no-hitter, but they were creating a constant buzz throughout the ballpark.

Santo struck out to open the eighth. Banks struck out, and Byron Browne went down swinging as well.

The buzz in the stands turned to cheers.

The Dodgers went down in order in the bottom of the eighth.

Koufax calmly removed his warm-up jacket and walked to the mound to a thunderous ovation. As if oblivious to the roar of the crowd, he calmly got Chris Krug to swing and miss strike three.

The roar became deafening.

With everyone in the stands on their feet, pinch hitter Joey Amalfitano went down swinging.

One out remained.

The crowd continued to cheer even louder until the announcement came over the public address system: "Now batting for pitcher Bob Hendley, Harvey Kuenn."

As if cued by a stern director, the once raucous crowd fell silent.

Up to the plate stepped Kuenn, a former batting champion of the American League who had a current batting average of .303.

Koufax reared back and let fly. Kuenn swung and missed. With his trademark wad of tobacco clearly visible in his right cheek, Kuenn spit on the ground and resumed his stance. Koufax threw again; Kuenn swung and missed again.

The crowd cheered even louder. Then the stadium took on the silence of a mausoleum.

Koufax put as much mustard as possible on his 113th pitch of the night, a blistering fastball that got Kuenn out swinging.

Catcher Jeff Torborg raced to the mound and embraced the dazed pitcher.

Sandy Koufax had just pitched a perfect game.

Jim Murray of the *Los Angeles Times* wrote after the game, "With the Babe Ruth Yankees, Sandy Koufax would probably have been the first undefeated pitcher in history."

Bob Hendley gave up only one hit all night, to Lou Johnson in the bottom of the seventh. It was the best game of his career, yet he went home without the W.

# WHY DID OUTFIELDER PETE GRAY PRESENT A STRANGE SIGHT ON A MAJOR LEAGUE BASEBALL DIAMOND IN 1945?

To play baseball on a major-league team is a dream that thousands of American boys have shared since the sport's inception. But when young Peter Wyshner of Nanticoke, Pennsylvania, announced to his friends and neighbors that he was going to audition as an outfielder for the 1945 St. Louis Browns of the American League, at least a few were surprised.

Why did it seem strange that this young man was intent on earning a position on the Browns' roster? It was because Wyshner had only one arm.

Even recruits with a standard body had a slim chance of becoming a fixture in the outfield for a big-league team. It defied logic for an average youngster with only one useable arm to even think that he had a chance to make the squad.

But Wyshner wasn't your average baseball player.

The 6-foot-1, 234-pound outfielder explained that, at age six, he fell off a farmer's wagon and his right arm was caught in the spokes. He had to be rushed to the hospital and, despite the skills of the surgeons in attendance, his arm had to be amputated above the elbow.

As a youngster he learned to catch a fly ball by using a glove without padding (which allowed him to grip the ball better) and, after catching it, to drop it under the stump of his right shoulder, grabbing it and throwing it to the correct base.

He also had to teach himself to bat left-handed and spent hours . . . days . . . years in practice. Eventually he developed enough skills to gain the attention of scouts.

By then he had changed his surname to Gray in order to avoid an ethnic association with (and possible discrimination because of) his former name.

He played for several years in the minors, where he racked up impressive statistics with a .333 batting average, 68 stolen bases, and even five home runs. So that he would be able to get a bat on the ball thrown by fastball pitchers, he used a rather light bat (35 ounces), starting his swing early to compensate for his disability. In 1945 he was signed by the Browns.

The timing for Gray could not have been better. The United States was in the last stages of World War II. Many pro players had traded their pinstripes for military uniforms. That left more room for people such as Pete Gray.

During the '45 season, Gray played in 77 games and batted .218.

The next year he no longer was a candidate for the majors, so he settled on a career of visiting handicapped veterans at Walter Reed General Hospital and became a welcome source of inspiration to those who had grown depressed because of serious wounds from the war.

Gray died on June 30, 2002, in his hometown at age 87.

"BASEBALL IS THE ONLY FIELD OF ENDEAVOR WHERE A MAN CAN SUCCEED THREE TIMES OUT OF TEN AND BE CONSIDERED A GOOD PERFORMER."

**TED WILLIAMS**

# WHY DID HANK GREENBERG ESPECIALLY RELISH HIS FINAL HOME RUN OF THE 1945 REGULAR SEASON?

A wise man once said that America never matured until December 7, 1941—the day that our nation was turned upside down by Japan's surprise attack on Pearl Harbor.

Major League Baseball, too, had to adjust to the impact of what President Franklin Roosevelt called the "Day of Infamy." World War II sent able-bodied men from the comfort of home to battlefields in Germany and Japan. Of those who enlisted in the US Army, Marine Corps, Navy, Air Corps, and Coast Guard, 428 were big-league baseball players who volunteered to serve overseas.

Because so many of the most talented players were no longer on major-league rosters, a lot of the nation feared that baseball would have to cancel its season. President Roosevelt himself put that fear to rest when he wrote a letter to Commissioner Kenesaw Mountain Landis, saying that the games should proceed for the "best of the country."

HANK GREENBERG, FAR RIGHT, AT THE 1937 ALL-STAR GAME.

Following the surrender of Germany on May 8, 1945, and the aftermath of the dropping of atomic bombs on Hiroshima and Nagasaki on August 6 and 9 of that same year, baseball players returned to their homes and were free to return to their former teams.

Included in the notable returning veterans was a powerful slugger for the Detroit Tigers, Henry Benjamin Greenberg.

Baseball still was battling to decide which teams would be playing in the World Series.

By September 30 of that year, Washington had a record of 87–67. But Detroit was still in the lead for the American League title.

Detroit had two games yet to play over the weekend against the St. Louis Browns. If the Tigers won just one of those games, the pennant would be theirs.

The first of the two games was rained out. The next day things did not look much better. Just minutes prior to the scheduled start time, the skies opened up and sent a heavy downpour onto Sportsman's Park in St. Louis. When the rain let up, the grounds crew quickly spread sand over the infield in order to make the diamond semi-playable. After a one-hour delay, the umpires allowed the game to start.

Detroit's starting pitcher was Virgil "Fire" Trucks, a right-hander fresh out of the military. St. Louis countered with seasoned veteran Nels Potter, who had posted a 2.47 ERA.

In the home half of the first, the Browns' Don Gutteridge and Lou Finney combined a double and a single to make the score 1–0 in favor of St. Louis.

One inning later, Detroit tied the score with the help of singles by James "Skeeter" Webb and Eddie Mayo. In the third, the Tigers pulled ahead on a pair of walks and a single by Paul Richards.

Detroit felt increasingly optimistic as the rain began again and showed no sign of letting up.

In the bottom half of the sixth, Trucks showed signs of weakness when he surrendered a double to Potter and walked Gutteridge. Manager Steve O'Neill had seen enough and called for a relief hurler. And he brought in a dandy–Hal

Newhouser (24 wins, 29 complete games, and that year's Most Valuable Player).

"Prince Hal" quickly retired the side.

His overpowering stuff did not last, however. In the seventh, Gene Moore doubled and Vern Stephens sent him home with the tying run.

The rain fell even harder.

The Tigers' anxieties turned to a full-blown depression when, in the bottom of the seventh, the Browns pulled ahead when Finney singled and George McQuinn sent him home with the go-ahead run. The score now was St. Louis 3, Detroit 2. And there was only one inning remaining.

Detroit came to bat in the top of the ninth. The Browns' fans were screaming at the umpires to call the game for two reasons: The fans wanted to get home out of the rain, and St. Louis would be declared the winner under the rules of baseball.

Harvey "Hub" Walker, batting for Newhouser, led off the top of the ninth with a pinch-hit single. Webb laid down a sacrifice bunt, but the Browns' McQuinn, in an attempt to force out Walker at second, threw too late. Both runners were safe. Mayo followed with a successful sacrifice bunt. Roger Cramer walked, loading the bases with only one out.

A hush fell over the crowd as big Hank Greenberg advanced toward the plate. Raising his 40-ounce bat high over his shoulder, Hammerin' Hank sent the first pitch deep toward the left field, appearing to part the rain and twilight. After the ball disappeared into the bleachers, the Tigers were ahead 6–3.

When Detroit's next pitcher retired the Browns to end the game in the ninth, the Tigers were the new American League champs.

Following the game, a beaming Hank Greenberg said to the gathering reporters in the locker room, "The best part of the home run was hearing later that some of the Washington players said, 'That dirty Jew bastard, he beat us again.' They were calling me all kinds of names behind my back, and now they had to pack up and go home, while we were going to the World Series."

**"THE GREAT THING ABOUT BASEBALL IS THERE'S A CRISIS EVERY DAY."**

GABE PAUL

# WHY DID THE NEW YORK YANKEES FIRE CASEY STENGEL FOLLOWING THE 1960 SEASON?

The answer to that question depends a lot on who you ask. At first blush it would appear that Charles Dillon "Casey" Stengel (also known as "the Ol' Perfessor") was the ideal candidate to lead ballplayers to heights theretofore unexpected in terms of their development on the field. He certainly achieved a remarkable record over his managerial career: 1,905 wins and 1,842 losses, for a winning percentage of .508.

Stengel managed the New York Yankees for 12 years, from 1949 through 1960. Under his direction, the club won 10 pennants and seven World Series, five of them consecutive. Stengel is the only manager to ever achieve that feat.

However, he did have a problem with team owners when he lost the 1960 Series with the club. By then he was 70 years old, and he was abruptly dismissed from the Yankees shortly after the final run crossed the plate. The Pirates'

**CASEY STENGEL'S FIRING BY THE YANKEES FOLLOWING THE 1960 WORLD SERIES MADE NATIONAL NEWS.**

second sacker, Bill Mazeroski, hit the game-winning homer in the last half of the ninth.

"They told me my services were no longer needed," Stengel said. "They wanted to put in a youth program." As an afterthought, he added, "I'll never make the mistake of being 70 again."

Stengel would go on to manage the Mets. In 1966, he was elected to the Hall of Fame.

He died in 1975 at the age of 85.

**"THE KEY TO BEING A GOOD MANAGER IS KEEPING THE PEOPLE WHO HATE ME AWAY FROM THOSE WHO ARE STILL UNDECIDED."**

CASEY STENGEL

# WHY ARE THE CAREERS OF BASEBALL MANAGERS SO OFTEN CUT SHORT?

The history of Major League Baseball is saturated with stories of outstanding managers who led teams to totally unexpected levels of success. Most often, however, the outlook for managers is that they eventually will be fired; they just don't know when.

Some say that managing a baseball team is the toughest job in all of professional sports. Why? Because the manager has limited involvement in the strategic management of the game. Other than rotating pitchers and changing defensive alignments, he can't change the batting order. He is judged primarily on how he motivates his players and rotates his pitchers. Owners can see pretty quickly if the manager is failing in either of these respects, where as an NFL coach, for example, may need several years to implement a new offensive scheme.

One of the bits of sage advice that seems to work for most skippers was passed along by Don Gutteridge, manager of the White Sox in the late 1960s. He urged outgoing managers to "leave three envelopes in the top desk drawer" for their replacement. For incoming managers, he had this advice: "When your team is in a slump and you don't know what to do, go to your desk and open the first envelope. If what you read does not solve your problem, go to the second envelope. Finally, the third."

A team was burdened by its losing ways. The new manager went to the desk drawer and pulled out envelope #1. Inside was a piece of paper with a simple message: "Blame it on your predecessor." At the press conference that afternoon, the new manager did just that.

After another week of more losses and sloppy play, pressure from the fans and the media continued. The new manager went to his desk and withdrew envelope #2. He read, "Write a new lineup."

The young manager did as the message instructed. Again, he saw no improvement in the team's performance. Some of the press were calling for the skipper to resign.

Finally, the media rumblings and fan resentment became far too intense, so the new manager returned to his desk and took out envelope #3. What he read this time was the simple message, in bold print, "Prepare three envelopes."

# WHY ARE SUCCESSFUL BASEBALL MANAGERS DIFFICULT TO FIND?

Every American male is convinced that he can outdo the professionals in three different endeavors: (1) running a hotel, (2) grilling a steak, and (3) managing a Major League Baseball team.

Why is it so difficult to find just the right manager for any given team?

When asked this question at one of his last press conferences, four-time manager of the Pittsburgh Pirates, Danny Murtaugh, responded forthrightly: "Why, certainly I'd like to have that fellow who hits a home run every time at bat, who strikes out every batter when he's pitching, who throws strikes to any base when he's playing the outfield, and who's always thinking about two innings ahead just what he'd do to baffle the other team. Ask any manager who wouldn't want a guy like that playing for him. The only trouble is to get him to put down his cup of beer and come down out of the stands and do these things."

# WHY WAS ROBERTO CLEMENTE DESCRIBED AS HAVING A "TOUCH OF ROYALTY"?

The shortest answer to this question may be "Because it's true."

To any fan who lived outside the city limits of Pittsburgh, this would be a strange observation. But in the real world, talent in and of itself is no guarantee of fame on the baseball diamond.

Among the acceptable criteria for stardom in Major League Baseball are more important considerations—the most important being the team's location.

Look at the household names that have come out of New York City as compared to players from smaller markets. One of the best examples of this unfair treatment came from the relatively small island of Puerto Rico.

His name was Roberto Clemente.

Actually, his full name was Roberto Enrique Clemente Walker, but a baseball scout shortened it because he found

LOU GEHRIG, JACKIE ROBINSON, AND ROBERTO CLEMENTE, IMMORTALIZED AT
THE BASEBALL HALL OF FAME.

it much easier to limit the number of letters spread out on
his evaluation report. As the talent of this recruit became
more apparent, however, it became easier for any observer
to recall the real name of this superb athlete.

Had ballet dancer Mikhail Baryshnikov elected to become
a professional baseball player, he would have played right
field like Roberto Clemente. That's how gracefully "the Great
One," as the media dubbed Clemente, executed his on-field
duties.

He did not exactly set the world on fire during his rookie
season in 1955 with a batting average of .255, although
he did draw attention with his routine of nabbing fly balls
with basket catches a la Willie Mays. In addition, he made a

howitzer-like throw back to the infield whenever a base runner dared to take an extra base following a hit.

He even showed an unorthodox approach to hitting. Instead of standing upright in the batter's box, the feisty Puerto Rican constantly moved his shoulders around in tiny circles as if he had spent the entire night on a bad mattress. Instead of waiting for a good pitch to hit, he would often swing at a pitch 10 inches outside the plate and send a sharp line drive to right.

As his career became more and more spectacular, even some of the local media became enthralled with Clemente's strange behavior. One of them was radio broadcaster Bob Prince, who over the air encouraged the fans to shout "Arriba! Arriba!" –Spanish for "Rise up!"

Throughout the years other commentators took up the spirit of those watching this rare talent. During the 1960 season, when the Pirates defeated the highly favored New York Yankees in the World Series, some sportswriters went so far as to label Clemente the most exciting player in baseball that year. He hit a sizzling .314, with 16 home runs and a club-leading 94 RBIs.

Respected baseball insiders such as writer Joe Falls of the *Detroit Free Press* felt that Clemente wrote the book on how to play right field.

"Clemente could field a ball in New York and throw a guy out in Pennsylvania," claimed veteran broadcaster Vin Scully.

That said, Clemente was not often given the accolades due to someone of his ability. Only in Pittsburgh did fans openly embrace this superstar. As a demonstration of their love and admiration of him, on July 25, 1970, Pirate fans honored him in a special ceremony before a home game. The famed right fielder returned their love for him when he said to his fans, "I was born in 1934 and again in 1955 when I came to Pittsburgh. I am thankful to say that I've had two lives."

Clemente's star shined the brightest during the 1971 World Series between the Pirates and the Baltimore Orioles. The Pirates' standout hit an astounding .414 during the seven-game Series. He slugged two doubles, a triple, and two home runs. He also played right field with a confidence that bordered on arrogance. Jerry Isenberg, a writer for the *Newark Star-Ledger*, observed, "After 17 major league seasons, Roberto Clemente is an overnight sensation."

Clemente guaranteed his place in Cooperstown on September 30, 1972, when he slammed a double to left-center field at Three Rivers Stadium against the New York Mets. It was the 3,000th hit of his illustrious career. Baseball enthusiasts still remember the image of Clemente standing on second base, waving his hat in response to the five-minute standing ovation by the fans at the ballpark.

On the morning of January 1, 1973, no Pirate fan was in the mood to celebrate anything, including the New Year.

Headlines throughout the nation told the shocking story: "Clemente Dies in Plane Crash."

News reports revealed that, the day before, the hero to many of his countrymen volunteered to board a DC-7 aircraft to help transfer 16,000 pounds of relief supplies to earthquake victims in Managua, Nicaragua. Shortly after takeoff, the plane burst into flames, banked sharply to the left, and plunged deep into the ocean.

Roberto Clemente was dead. No one ever found his body.

He was only 38 years old.

During his 18 years with the Pittsburgh Pirates, Clemente topped the .300 mark 13 times, won four National League batting crowns, batted .317, hit 240 home runs, and knocked in 1,305 runs. He won 12 Golden Glove awards, was selected 12 times to the All-Star team, and was voted the National League MVP in 1966.

His epitaph on a memorial plaque in Puerto Rico reads, "I want to be remembered as a ballplayer who gave all he had to give."

When baseball commissioner Bowie Kuhn heard about Clemente's death, he described the premier right fielder with just eight words: "He had about him a touch of royalty."

That was Roberto Clemente.

*Arriba!*

# WHY DID SOMEONE NICKNAMED "THE BIRD" CAUSE A NATIONAL SENSATION IN THE AMERICAN LEAGUE?

Most baseball fans of any generation are familiar with a third sacker from Cincinnati named "Charlie Hustle," an outfielder for the old Dodgers known as "the Duke," and a slugger from New York called "the Babe." But have you ever heard of a major leaguer lovingly referenced as "the Bird"?

Back in 1976 there was one such person. He was a pitcher for the Detroit Tigers, and his real name was Mark Steven Fidrych.

Why was he given such a nickname? He was a tall, lanky kid from the eastern US who reminded fans of Big Bird, a regular character on the popular national television show Sesame Street. The show was designed for children, but the antics of the character drew a huge adult audience as well.

Both Fidrych and his television namesake were loveable characters who were unafraid to break the rules of acceptable behavior as long as nobody got hurt. Everyone who was

# Fidrych makes his mark

By Dave Anderson

New York Times News Service

NEW YORK—His mother was shopping one day when Mark Fidrych, then about 3 years old, suddenly disappeared from her side.

"We found him in the front window," his mother recalled.

"He had crawled into the front window of Sears, Roebuck."

Even at that age Mark "The Bird" Fidrych was gravitating to the front window. Monday night Mark Fidrych crawled into the front window of the ABC television network and into the heart of everybody who watched him. Mark Fidrych is a 21-year-old rookie righthander for the Detroit Tigers with an 9-1 won-lost record, a rock-star hairdo and a "You Know Me, Al" manner.

If he were a racehorse, his breeding would be a cross between rock singer Roger Daltrey and Ring Lardner. He talks to the baseball before he pitches. He smoothes the mound with his hands as if he were stroking a puppy. He cheers his teammates when they make a good play, he consoles them when they make a bad play. Because of his natural enthusiasm, he communicates with the fans perhaps as no other athlete has.

He was the primary attraction for 47,835 customers at Tiger Stadium Monday night and stopped the New York Yankees, 5-1, on seven hits. Saturday, 51,032 turned out in Detroit for his first major league shutout, a 4-0 four-hitter against Baltimore.

PART OF THE chemistry of Mark Fidrych's appeal might be that he's making only $16,500, the major-league minimum. People not only can identify with him easier than they can with the

Mark Fidrych
UPI Telephoto

millionaire athletes, but people also WANT to identify with a ballplayer who is driving a Dodge Colt instead of a Rolls-Royce.

"And he's sweating out the payments," his mother Virginia was saying now over the telephone from their Northboro, Mass. home. "He had a '69 Chevy, a yellow two-door, but he didn't think it would get him to Florida for Spring training so he bought the new car. He's good with cars. He's always tinkering with them. And when something isn't working, he talks to the car just like he talks to the baseball. That's the way my Marky is. He's always loved baseball. When he was small, he used to go to bed with his baseball hat on and with his glove under the mattress.

"When he was little he was in the cupboard all the time," his mother said. "I remember he once poured Comet cleanser on my maple coffee table in the living room and rubbed it in. I thought he ruined it, but it was all right."

"Things are always happening to him," his father Paul, an assistant principal of a junior high school, said. "In school once, he accidentally bounced an acorn into a teacher's coffee cup. Another time he rolled down a hill into a fire at the bottom. But he was all right."

"HE ALWAYS had a good arm," said Billy McAfee, a 23-year-old neighbor. "When we had our little backyard wars, he threw rocks and snowballs harder than anybody. But he really got into baseball after the Tigers signed him."

Disdaining college as "not my bag," Mark Fidrych emerged from Algonquin High School as the 10th-round choice of the Tigers in the 1974 draft. His antics might have turned off some baseball people. But his fastball turned them on. After the Tigers' general manager, Jim Campbell, scouted their Evansville, Ind. farm team in the American Association last season, his advice to Mark Fidrych was, "Don't let anybody change you." When the 6-3 pitcher with the blond curls arrived at Spring training, Tiger Manager, Ralph Houk, had been alerted that Mark Fidrych is different.

"I just hope Marky doesn't change," his mother was saying now. "He sent me a dozen red roses for my birthday two weeks ago. I put one of the roses in the Bible he gave me for Christmas and when he phoned, I told him, 'Marky, please don't change.' He told me he wouldn't."

**MARK "THE BIRD" FIDRYCH CERTAINLY MADE A MARK DURING HIS BRIEF MAJOR LEAGUE BASEBALL CAREER.**

blessed to see both of them in action knew instantly that they wanted to show you a good time.

In 1976, Detroit was not a fan-friendly team that overflowed with superstars who could draw huge attendances. There was one exception, however: Fidrych, the 6-foot-3, 175-pound pitching phenom.

Fidrych made the Tigers' squad but had limited service as a pitcher until May 15, when he held the Cleveland Indians to a mere two hits and earned a complete game victory.

It was a series of unusual antics while pitching that got the Bird the most attention. For instance, he actually talked to the ball while on the mound. Fans watched him hold the ball in his right hand and give it a pointed message: "Now, come on, ball, be good. Don't get hit." He also walked around the mound, patting down the dirt and refusing the groundskeepers access to "his territory."

Following the games he won, the energetic right-hander would emerge from the dugout and run around the inside of the entire ballpark, shaking hands with every fan within reach.

People began to fill to the brim every stadium in which he pitched. He was becoming a national celebrity. He also became the most effective hurler on the staff, racking up a 12–6 record, and was a runaway selection for Rookie of the Year.

Tiger fans and the remainder of the baseball world were awaiting spring training, just to see what new levels of excitement he could offer to everyone in the sellout crowds in Tiger Stadium.

The 1977 season began quite well for young Mark, although he was not the sensation he had proven to be the year before. An injury to his throwing arm and a torn rotator cuff limited his appearances, so he ended the season with a 6–4 record.

At age 29 his career was over and Mark knew it. He moved to a 107-acre farm in Northborough, Massachusetts.

He married his sweetheart, Ann, with whom he had a daughter, Jessica.

He settled down to life as a farmer until April 13, 2009, when he was found dead, lying beneath his 10-wheel dump truck due to an accident that caused the truck to collapse on him.

It may be a safe bet that no one in baseball left such a powerful impact on the game in such a short time as Mark "the Bird" Fidrych.

"THERE ARE THREE TYPES OF BASEBALL PLAYERS:
THOSE WHO MAKE IT HAPPEN,
THOSE WHO WATCH IT HAPPEN,
AND THOSE WHO WONDER WHAT HAPPENS."
TOMMY LASORDA

# WHY WAS MARK MCGWIRE'S 62ND HOME RUN ABOUT MORE THAN BREAKING A RECORD?

On September 8, 1998, baseball was still in a funk.

Less than four years earlier, players and club owners had reached an impasse in labor negotiations. As a result, the last half of the '94 season—and that year's World Series—had been canceled.

Cooler heads eventually prevailed, and the next season began on time. But hostilities from previous fights continued. Players blamed owners for problems with salaries; owners blamed players for failure to give 100 percent while on the field.

In 1998, one man—a towering 6-foot-5, 225-pound first baseman for the St. Louis Cardinals—reinvigorated the game and completely turned the baseball universe upside down. He was threatening to surpass a humble left-handed slugger from Hibbing, Minnesota, named Roger Maris for the single-season home run record. As an added pressure, McGwire was being chased by Sammy Sosa, an outfielder for the Cubs.

The pivotal game of the year came on September 8, a matchup between the Cardinals and Cubs. McGwire had been sitting on 61 home runs. Sosa, the right fielder for the Cubs that evening, was only three homers behind.

From the reports given by the Cardinals organization, outside of Busch Stadium police arrested 27 scalpers who were seeking $500 apiece for one of the sold-out seats. Others used more creative approaches to snag a seat or earn a few dollars. One man held high a homemade sign. On one side it read "I have six months to live; I need a ticket." On the other side it read "Will trade kidney for a ticket."

THOUGH TAINTED BY HIS SUBSEQUENT ADMISSION OF STEROID USE, BASEBALL FANS WERE STILL CAPTIVATED BY MARK MCGWIRE'S PURSUIT OF ROGER MARIS'S HOME RUN RECORD, WHICH MCGWIRE SUCCEEDED IN TOPPING ON SEPTEMBER 8, 1998.

Inside the packed stadium were the children of the late Roger Maris. Mrs. Maris, owing in part to hectic pressure from the media, was resting in a hospital following an attack of exhaustion. Sitting near the Maris family were former Cardinal icons Stan Musial, Ozzie Smith, Lou Brock, and Red Schoendienst. Sitting behind were McGwire's former wife (from whom he had been divorced for several years) along with her new husband.

Reportedly, more people than had viewed any of the World Series games the previous year were glued to their television sets, hoping to see history made. When McGwire first took the batter's box, he sent the crowd into a collective moan by hitting a weak ground ball for an out.

Chicago was nursing a 2–0 lead until the bottom of the fourth. Fans in the stadium and the millions watching on national television remained fixed as the red-haired slugger wearing number 25 strode to the plate.

They would not be disappointed this time.

At 8:18 p.m., on the first pitch from Cubs hurler Steve Trachsel, McGwire took one of his Paul Bunyan–like swings and sent a line drive toward the left-field wall. Veteran telecaster Mike Shannon screamed into the microphone, "Swing and shot into the corner. It might make it! There it is . . . sixty-two, folks! It just got over the left-field wall in the corner. And we have a new home run champion. A new Sultan of Swat! It's Mark McGwire."

The ball barely made it just inches over the fence—not much compared to the gargantuan hits that had already made "Big Mac" a legend. It was also the shortest home run he would hit all summer.

The 43,688 fans who filled the stadium plus the millions of television viewers throughout the United States screamed with delight. Fireworks shot from behind the left-field wall. A giant banner was unfurled over the center-field scoreboard that read "Mark McGwire – 62."

Sammy Sosa rushed in from his outfield position and warmly embraced his friend. McGwire then spotted the Maris family seated near the dugout. He hopped the fence and hugged the children and whispered fond words to each of them.

It was a moment that surpassed any preconceived plan designed by a professional PR agent.

A groundskeeper at Busch Stadium—22-year-old Tim Forneris—had placed himself behind the left-field fence. When the home run ball sailed over the 330-foot mark, young Forneris saw the ball land less than 15 feet away. The college student ran for the ball, and, as the fireworks were blasting away and the streamers hit the field, he placed the ball (immediately worth at least $1 million) into his jacket pocket.

When he finally got to see the new home run champion, Forneris held the ball in his outstretched hand and said,

"Mr. McGwire, I have something that I think belongs to you." Someone asked him why he didn't keep the ball and sell it. The young groundskeeper replied, "It's not mine to keep. McGwire just lost it. It's his. I just got to bring it home."

Author's note: With all of the controversy that has dogged Mark McGwire over the years since, someone might ask why this story is worthy of being included in this volume. My answer is this: That night, the game reached beyond the super salaries and inflated egos too often associated with baseball. Instead, it involved the age-old, one-on-one drama of a powerful slugger facing a crafty pitcher. It showed a man breaking one of the sport's most sacred records, then taking time to embrace the children of the previous record holder. It featured a young college student giving away a baseball valued at over $1 million because, as he said, "It was the right thing to do."

On September 8, 1998, every baseball fan, once again, was able to see the heart of the game.

# WHY IS MAJOR LEAGUE BASEBALL EXEMPT FROM ANTITRUST LAWS?

Baseball is the only sport not subject to federal antitrust laws. Here's why.

In 1922, the Supreme Court ruled that antitrust laws apply only to interstate commerce and that baseball is a state-centered business, even though players and teams must cross state lines to travel to opponents' ballparks and play games.

This antitrust exemption, which allows Major League Baseball to operate as a legal monopoly, has resulted in the sport having fewer franchise locations than the National Football League, National Basketball Association, and National Hockey League, and in owners having more control over player contracts.

The exemption was tested back in 1969 when a heralded outfielder for the St. Louis Cardinals, Curt Flood, challenged the MLB's reserve clause, which bound players to their teams indefinitely and gave players no say in being traded or sold.

The Cardinals wanted to send Flood to the Phillies, a club he had no desire to join. He argued that players had the right to offer their skills to any other team once a contract was completed. He lost in court but paved the way for Andy Messersmith and David McNally to get a different outcome some six years later—and for Congress to pass the Curt Flood Act in 1998. This act offers major-league baseball players the same antitrust protection that other professional athletes enjoy.

If the MLB lost its antitrust exemption through some decision by a court, the effect on big-league baseball would be minimal in today's market. Repeal mostly would open up new markets for play and allow more local games to be televised. While the initial exemption may have made a lot of sense as written by Justice Oliver Wendell Holmes a century ago, it has far less impact on the sport today.

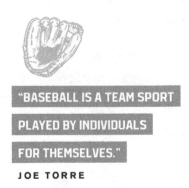

"BASEBALL IS A TEAM SPORT PLAYED BY INDIVIDUALS FOR THEMSELVES."

JOE TORRE

# WHY ARE FEWER AFRICAN AMERICAN ENTERING THE ROSTERS OF MAJOR LEAGUE BASEBALL?

Throughout these United States, most Americans consider baseball the national sport. A growing number of sports fans, however, may challenge this claim by presenting some recent statistics.

In 1981, 18.7 percent of MLB players were African American. In 2019, the percentage has dropped to less than half that number.

The decline starts well before the majors. According to the National Sporting Goods Association, nine million kids between the ages of 7 and 17 played baseball in 2002. By 2013, that figure was 41 percent lower.

As participation throughout the nation declined, youth leagues and teams had to merge or to shut down, limiting both exposure and access to the sport.

Another factor is that many young people today regard the NFL and the NBA as "cooler" because these games have more ongoing action and active scoring.

Finally, there is the dimension of preparation time required. In MLB, even the best players must spend several years in minor-league baseball perfecting their skills while riding buses, staying in cheap hotels, and eating too much fast food. The price may be too high for most young athletes to get to "the show." In short, when an NFL prospect or an NBA prospect arrives in rookie camp, he has a far better chance to make the roster by the start of the new season.

With the increasing number of life-altering injuries in the NFL and the fact that the NBA limits the number of active players (15) for each franchise during the playing season, chances are that the percentage of African American players will increase in Major League Baseball. The league, for its part, is trying to enliven the sport's conservative image and recruit more baseball executives and managers of color.

# WHY IS MAJOR LEAGUE BASEBALL'S ALL-TIME HITS LEADER NOT IN THE HALL OF FAME?

This sounds impossible, but it's true. It seems especially bizarre when you consider the fact that this baseball icon racked up other impressive numbers as well.

The all-time hits record belongs to a scrappy infielder named Peter Edward Rose, also known around all of baseball as "Charlie Hustle" because of his aggressive play. He amassed 4,256 hits across 24 seasons of play.

Perhaps that record should, in and of itself, guarantee his place in Cooperstown. Alas, neither you nor any other fan will see a plaque bearing his name hanging among those for other giants of the game on the wall when you visit the Hall of Fame.

According to many baseball experts, his exclusion seems even more ridiculous when you consider that this switch-hitting enthusiast is also the record holder for the number of games played (3,562), at bats (14,053), plate appearances

(15,890), and singles (3,215). Today, most baseball experts agree that none of these figures will probably ever be surpassed by any future player who is fortunate to don a pair of cleats.

During his nearly quarter century of being one of the game's top performers, Rose won three batting titles, was elected to 17 All-Star teams, and won three World Series, an MVP Award, a Rookie of the Year Award, two Gold Glove Awards, a Silver Slugger Award, and the Roberto Clemente Award. He was also named to Major League Baseball's All-Century Team in 1999.

All of these notable records and awards should have made him a sure-fire candidate to become a first-ballot Hall of Famer. Alas, all of this potential disappeared into thin air in 1989 when then-commissioner A. Bartlett (Bart) Giamatti declared Rose to be permanently ineligible based upon overwhelming evidence that this outstanding athlete gambled on baseball games while managing for the Reds during his second stint with the team (1984–1989).

Commissioner Giamatti did not easily arrive at his decision to banish this flashy superstar from the game. Prior to all of the gaming hoopla, he was a solid Pete Rose fan.

Shortly after he made this heartbreaking decision, Giamatti, a former president of Yale University, suddenly died from a heart attack at age 51.

Throughout the investigation by Giamatti and others, Rose continually denied the accusations of improper gambling. But in 2004, 15 years after his banishment from the game, Rose admitted to betting on baseball as well as the Reds. He maintained, however, that he had never bet against the Reds.

Baseball fans to this day debate whether Rose has been treated unfairly, especially in light of his remarkable achievements on the baseball diamond. Many applaud the decision of the commissioner by insisting that fans should never suspect that the outcome of any baseball game is already determined before the first pitch is delivered. While respecting the unequaled accomplishments of a man who dazzled the baseball world with his all-out zest for winning, they argue that if we allow gamblers to dictate (or even to contribute) to the outcome of a game, the game itself may be considered no more of an honest display of talent than is professional wrestling.

# WHY DOES MAJOR LEAGUE BASEBALL INSIST ON KEEPING A COMMISSIONER TO SUPERVISE THE SPORT?

This goes back to the days of the National Commission—the ruling body formed in 1903 to make peace between the two existing leagues: the National League and the upstart American League.

The commission comprised the two league presidents and a chairman. Their responsibilities were primarily to run meetings and to mediate disputes. Chairman August "Gary" Herrmann, president of the Cincinnati Reds, was the de facto head of MLB, but Ban Johnson, president of the American League, was the commission's driving force.

The Black Sox Scandal, in which eight members of the Chicago White Sox were accused of taking bribes to lose the 1919 World Series, strained relations between club owners and Johnson. The dynamic led to a structural change in governance: namely, that a single commissioner with no previous association with the game would be elected by the owners to oversee all aspects of the sport and to make certain that gamblers did not corrupt the integrity of the game.

To date, MLB has had ten commissioners. Kenesaw Mountain Landis, a gruff-looking federal judge in Chicago, was named MLB's inaugural commissioner in 1920. In that capacity, he expelled eight members of the 1919 White Sox (hence the name of the film *Eight Men Out*). He remained commissioner until his death in 1944.

Landis was followed by Albert "Happy" Chandler (1945–1951), a Southerner who oversaw baseball's breaking of the color barrier; Ford Frick (1951–1965), a former sportswriter

FORD FRICK CHATTING WITH PRESIDENT FRANKLIN ROOSEVELT. FRICK IS TO FDR'S IMMEDIATE LEFT.

CURRENT (2020) BASEBALL COMMISSIONER ROB MANFRED.

who had served as a ghostwriter for Babe Ruth and who insisted on separating Roger Maris' single-season home run record (61), achieved in a 162-game season, from the record his former client set (60) during a 154-game schedule; Lieutenant General William Eckert (1965–1968), a compromise choice whom writers dubbed "the Unknown Soldier"; Bowie Kuhn (1969–1984), whose tenure was characterized by labor strikes, the dawn of free agency, and record gains in attendance at ballparks and in the size of television contracts; Peter Ueberroth (1984–1989), who presided over an era of collusion among owners to depress players' salaries; A. Bartlett Giamatti (1989), who died from a heart attack at age 51 after only five months on the job, and eight days after banishing Pete Rose for gambling activities; Fay Vincent (1989–1992), Giamatti's deputy, who suspended Yankees owner George Steinbrenner for the 1990 season for conspiring with gamblers in order to obtain scandalous information on player Dave Winfield; Allan (Bud) Selig (1992–2015), former owner of the Milwaukee Brewers who served as executive council chairman from 1992 to 1998 and thereafter as commissioner, and who presided over numerous changes in corporate structure, resulting in unprecedented growth of MLB; and Rob Manfred (2015–present), who has helped baseball through numerous economic changes and improved the league's competitive balance.

# WHY DO TWO MAJOR LEAGUE BASEBALL TEAMS KEEP A HUMIDOR AS PART OF THEIR REGULAR EQUIPMENT?

When we think of the standard equipment always on tap for big-league baseball games, hundreds of baseballs might come to mind first. Then there's one set of uniforms for home games, another for away games, and still another for special occasions. And these are just some of the basics. For two other clubs, there's yet another expense—a humidor.

That's something that certainly was never expected when Abner Doubleday equipped his first baseball team in the 1800s.

As any high school science student is aware, once a baseball is removed from the usual environment of "standard" humidity, it loses some of its moisture and becomes lighter in weight. The difference may not be much, but there is a difference nonetheless. Both Arizona and Colorado are states marked by low humidity. As a result, when heavy hitters join the rosters in Denver and Phoenix, sluggers and their fans delight to see their home runs soar farther than they would at other venues.

But no one wants that benefit extended to the visiting team—hence the addition of humidors for baseball storage. Does the addition of a humidor solve the problem? Let the facts speak for themselves. From 1995 through the 2001 season, National League pitchers at Coors Field recorded a horrific earned run average of 6.50; that was noticeably higher than the 4.37 recorded by clubs in every other location within the league.

In 2002, when a humidor was introduced as standard equipment for the Colorado Rockies, home run production at the mile-high stadium dropped 25 percent during the season.

That statistic was enough to convince the powers that be for the Arizona Diamondbacks to also add a humidor to their list of "must have" equipment during their home games.

# WHY WERE SOME OF THE COLORADO ROCKIES' SLUGGERS CALLED THE "BLAKE STREET BOMBERS"?

Baseball fans who lived in Colorado during the early 1990s should recall a quintet of heavy hitters known as the "Blake Street Bombers." As the designation suggests, these members of the Colorado Rockies smacked the cover off of the ball (an exaggeration, of course) in the pre-humidor days when hits were more likely to sail over the outfield walls of Coors Field and into the thin air that engulfs the stadium and the city.

The location of the baseball park—on Blake Street, in Denver's Lower Downtown (LoDo) neighborhood—made for convenient alliteration.

The five stars who earned such a coveted title were Dante Bichette, Ellis Burks, Andres Galarraga, Vinny Castilla, and Larry Walker.

# WHY WAS THE PITCHER'S MOUND LOWERED FROM 15 INCHES TO 10 INCHES ABOVE THE BASELINE, WHERE IT HAS STAYED SINCE 1969?

One of the truths of Major League Baseball is that fans throughout the land obviously prefer watching offense as opposed to defense.

While so-called experts in the field talk in glowing terms about the excitement of a pitchers' duel, the average fan gets more worked up about base hits and home runs.

That became most apparent in 1968 when two hurlers dominated the news. The first was fire-balling Bob Gibson of the St. Louis Cardinals, who routinely sent opposing hitters back to the dugout as he racked up an amazing season record of 22–9. He was the obvious winner of the Cy Young Award and the National League's Most Valuable Player Award. He also demonstrated his powerful domination later that year in the World Series.

His American League rival for pitching excellence that same year was another right-hander, Denny McLain of Detroit. While McLain had his share of strikeouts, of more significance to the general population was the fact that he was inching toward 30 wins in one season—an accomplishment unmatched by any pitcher for decades. Actually, he won 31 games that season as he led his Tigers to the World Series.

These weren't the only pitching sensations that year, but they grabbed the headlines.

A subtopic on many sports talk shows was the rather anemic hitting in both leagues. During the '68 season, the collective ERA for MLB was 2.98, the lowest in the previous half century and the lowest since 1901.

In fact, only one hitter in the American League broke .300 that year: Carl Yastrzemski won the league's batting title with a .301 average. Good, but certainly far from the number to which fans had grown accustomed.

Baseball fans showed their lack of enthusiasm in the clearest way possible. They preferred to watch games on TV as opposed to filling ballparks in person. Major League Baseball responded by lowering the pitcher's mound by five inches, thereby reducing the strike zone and generating more offense for fans bored by the "Year of the Pitcher."

# WHY ARE POSITION PLAYERS PITCHING MORE FREQUENTLY THESE DAYS?

Modern-day bullpens are assuming heavier workloads as starting pitchers rack up fewer innings. As a result, when a game gets out of hand—which means, in the minds of viewers, that it is "already won" by one side or the other—the losing team may elect to send a position player to the mound in lieu of calling in a relief pitcher. No one wants that pitcher to waste his talent or possibly injure himself in what would be regarded as a "mop-up" role.

Quite possibly the best position player to be brought into a game as an impromptu reliever was a former American League slugger named Rocky Colavito. He had a cannon for an arm. In August of 1958 he pitched three no-hit innings of relief for the Cleveland Indians. A decade later, at the end of his career, he took the mound for the New York Yankees and pitched two scoreless innings.

In 2011, position players pitched only eight times across the MLB season. In 2018, that number jumped to 65. With an increase in the number of position players taking the mound as relievers, some baseball fans fear that big-league baseball might be tempted to increase the number of players allowed on a team's roster.

"THOSE OLD BALLPARKS ARE LIKE CATHEDRALS IN AMERICA. WE DON'T HAVE BIG OLD GOTHIC CATHEDRALS LIKE THEY DO IN EUROPE. BUT WE GOT BASEBALL PARKS."

**JIMMY BUFFETT**

# WHY DID THE HOUSTON COLT .45S CHANGE THEIR NAME TO THE ASTROS IN 1965?

After just three seasons, the team known as the Houston Colt .45s changed its name to the Astros, to coincide with the new home ballpark. The Astrodome was the first indoor stadium and was referred to by journalists and civic boosters alike as the "Eighth Wonder of the World."

Another reason for the change was that the nickname Colt .45s symbolized a bygone era. The new team name represented a transition to the future, as the city had become the location of NASA's Manned Spaceflight Center. Congress renamed it the Lyndon B. Johnson Space Center in February 1973, a month following the death of the 36th US president, who was a native of Texas.

# WHY DID SO MANY BALLPARKS BUILT IN THE 1960S, '70S, AND '80S HAVE ARTIFICIAL PLAYING SURFACES INSTEAD OF NATURAL GRASS?

The simple answer to that question makes sense when you consider the times. Because baseball fields built during this time span were funded mostly by local and state governments and designed to accommodate both baseball and football, as well as other types of events such as concerts, rodeos, and even tractor pulls, those facilities used Astroturf and other types of artificial surfaces to help minimize maintenance costs.

Such ballparks were the Astrodome (Houston), Busch Stadium (St. Louis), Riverfront Stadium (Cincinnati), Three Rivers Stadium (Pittsburgh), Veterans Stadium (Philadelphia), Kauffman Stadium (Kansas City), Olympic Stadium (Montreal), Exhibition Stadium (Toronto), the Kingdome (Seattle), Hubert H. Humphrey Metrodome (Minneapolis), Rogers Centre (Toronto), and Tropicana Field (St. Petersburg). Among those aesthetically forgettable venues, Rogers Centre and Tropicana Field remain in use by MLB teams.

Although they were less expensive to maintain than natural grass, the artificial playing surfaces were much harder than grass, often hard as concrete. Batted balls, therefore, bounced higher than on natural surfaces, forcing both outfielders and infielders to position themselves farther back than on grass, and requiring fielders to possess stronger throwing arms. And the seams between pieces of turf sometimes caused fielders to catch their spikes and become injured.

"BASEBALL, IT IS SAID, IS ONLY A GAME.
TRUE. AND THE GRAND CANYON IS ONLY
A HOLE IN ARIZONA. NOT ALL HOLES,
OR GAMES, ARE CREATED EQUAL."
GEORGE WILL

# WHY DO THE ST. LOUIS CARDINALS HAVE SUCH A LARGE FOLLOWING OF FANS DESPITE BEING IN ONLY THE 19TH LARGEST METROPOLITAN AREA?

Until the Dodgers and the Giants announced their move from New York to California in 1957, the St. Louis Cardinals were the only team west of Milwaukee except for the Kansas City Athletics. Its geographic footprint was huge.

In addition, the club was blessed with the powerful signal of radio station KMOX as well as a strong network of radio (and later TV) affiliates in the lower Midwest, South, and West.

It also helped that the team was constantly in contention for the pennant thanks, in part, to the dynamic career of Stan "the Man" Musial (1939–1963).

If a family went to a weekend series at Busch Stadium, they would see hundreds of cars parked in lots bearing license plates from perhaps 10 states—exemplifying the wide reach of Cardinals baseball.

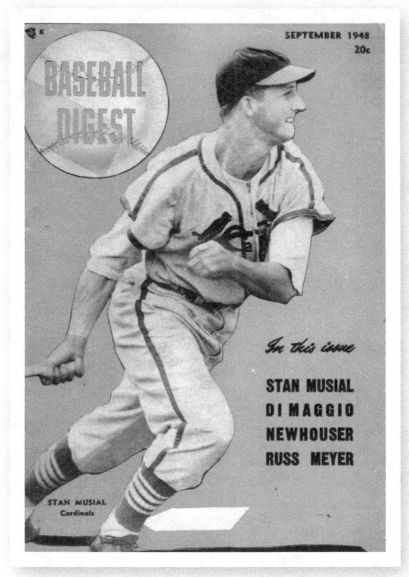

STAN MUSIAL'S PLAY HELPED PUT THE ST. LOUIS CARDINALS IN THE NATIONAL
SPOTLIGHT FROM 1941 TO 1963.

# WHY DID THE BLACK SOX SCANDAL OF 1919 OCCUR?

Exactly how eight Chicago White Sox players conspired to throw the 1919 World Series in exchange for payments from gamblers remains unclear. What is beyond doubt, however, is that players felt underpaid by Sox owner Charles Comiskey and jumped at the opportunity to make more money for themselves and their families, even if it meant violating the law and threatening the integrity of the sport they played for a living.

Arnold "Chick" Gandil, a first baseman for the team, masterminded the scandal. The other players participating were Oscar "Happy" Felsch, Eddie Cicotte, "Shoeless" Joe Jackson, Fred McMullin, Charles "Swede" Risberg, George "Buck" Weaver, and Claude "Lefty" Williams.

In a nutshell, the scandal took place when the heavily favored White Sox played the Cincinnati Reds and accepted financial kickbacks from a gaming syndicate led by Arnold Rothstein.

SHOELESS JOE JACKSON EVEN *LOOKS* SHIFTY IN THIS PHOTO FROM 1917.

The White Sox purposely lost the Series, taking eight games to do it. The players each received $5,000 or more.

Rumors circulated among seasoned fans that something was wrong with the Series. Their protests spurred growing doubt that the games were played on the up-and-up. Eventually the law took its course, and on June 27, 1921, following a grand jury investigation, a trial began in the Cook County courthouse.

Although the players were acquitted of wrongdoing in a court of law, baseball commissioner Kenesaw Mountain Landis, a former federal judge, issued a lifetime ban to each of the players involved in the affair.

Eliot Asinof's book *Eight Men Out* is a factual account of the scandal. The book was published in 1963 and was adapted into a movie in 1988.

**"A BASEBALL GAME IS SIMPLY A NERVOUS BREAKDOWN DIVIDED INTO NINE INNINGS."**
**EARL WILSON**

# WHY HASN'T MARVIN MILLER, THE LATE HEAD OF THE MAJOR LEAGUE BASEBALL PLAYERS ASSOCIATION, BEEN INDUCTED INTO THE HALL OF FAME?

Perhaps, as ex-MLB pitcher Jim Bouton, author of *Ball Four*, a diary of his 1969 season with the Seattle Pilots, put it back in 2008, "Marvin Miller kicked their butts and took power away from the baseball establishment."

Bouton was giving the unvarnished truth about the dislike the "Lords of Baseball" had for the Brooklyn-born labor leader who, early in his career, had been the United Steelworkers' chief economist and labor negotiator. He served as the executive director of the MLBPA from 1966 to 1982.

Former Dodgers broadcaster Red Barber called Miller one of the three most important figures in baseball history (Babe Ruth and Jackie Robinson being the others). Members of the Hall of Fame's Veterans Committee, which included owners, ex-players, and writers, didn't see it that way despite Miller's role in eliminating the reserve clause and shifting the balance of power from the owners to the players following a century of exploitation.

Under Miller's leadership, the average annual salary for a big-league player increased from $19,000 to more than $240,000 and the MLBPA became the country's strongest labor union.

Some 18 months before his death at the age of 95 in 2012, after learning that his bid for the Hall of Fame had failed again and would not be reconsidered for another 18 months, Miller wrote to the Veterans Committee to ask that he no longer be considered for the honor. Members of his family have echoed his sentiments in writing.

"CATCHING A FLY BALL IS A PLEASURE, BUT KNOWING WHAT TO DO WITH IT AFTER YOU CATCH IT IS A BUSINESS."

TOMMY HENRICH

# WHY IS THE AMERICAN LEAGUE CHAMPIONSHIP SERIES TROPHY NAMED FOR WILLIAM HARRIDGE?

The trophy honors the service of William (Will) Harridge. president of the American League from 1931 to 1959.

WILLIAM HARRIDGE, AMERICAN LEAGUE PRESIDENT FROM 1931 TO 1959.

Harridge (1883–1971), a Chicago native, began his career as a railway clerk and later became secretary to Byron Bancroft "Ban" Johnson, who was president of the American League from its inception in 1901 until 1927.

Harridge's most famous ruling took place in 1951 when Bill Veeck, owner of the St. Louis Browns, signed a 3-foot-7, 65-pound dwarf named Eddie Gaedel who made only one plate appearance in August of that year, drawing a four-pitch walk. Harridge contended that Veeck was making a mockery of the game and, on the very next day, canceled Gaedel's contract.

The Veterans Committee elected Harridge to Cooperstown immortality in 1972.

"THEY SAY SOME OF MY STARS DRINK WHISKEY. BUT I HAVE FOUND THAT THE ONES WHO DRINK MILKSHAKES DON'T WIN MANY BALL GAMES."
CASEY STENGEL

# WHY IS THE NATIONAL LEAGUE CHAMPIONSHIP SERIES TROPHY NAMED FOR WARREN GILES?

The trophy honors the service of Warren Giles, president of the National League from 1951 to 1969.

Giles (1896–1979), a western Illinois native, spent more than 30 years in MLB management. As president of the National League, he oversaw the relocation of the Boston Braves (to Milwaukee), the Brooklyn Dodgers (to Los Angeles), and the New York Giants (to San Francisco). On his watch, the National League signed more African American and Latino players than the American League.

Giles was elected to the Hall of Fame in 1979.

WARREN GILES, NATIONAL LEAGUE PRESIDENT FROM 1951 TO 1969.

# WHY IS THE NATIONAL BASEBALL HALL OF FAME'S ANNUAL AWARD TO A BROADCASTER CALLED THE FORD C. FRICK AWARD?

Each year since 1978, the National Baseball Hall of Fame has honored a broadcaster "for major contributions to baseball." It's a cherished honor named for Ford C. Frick, who served as MLB's third commissioner from 1951 to 1965.

According to the Hall of Fame, Frick "helped foster the relationship between radio and the game of baseball." The first two recipients of the Frick Award were Mel Allen and Red Barber, for their years of calling games for the New York Yankees and the Brooklyn Dodgers, respectively.

Prior to becoming commissioner, Frick was a respected baseball writer who made a name for himself as Babe Ruth's ghostwriter.

Frick Award winners are sometimes referred to as "Hall of Famers." But that designation is technically inaccurate; winners of the Frick Award have no plaques adorning the main gallery in Cooperstown. Instead, a living honoree gives a speech during the induction weekend, and his name is added to a plaque in the Hall's library.

Regardless, no broadcaster would turn down the opportunity to just be considered for the Ford C. Frick Award.

"MORE THAN ANY OTHER AMERICAN SPORT, BASEBALL CREATES THE MAGNETIC, ADDICTIVE ILLUSION THAT IT CAN ALMOST BE UNDERSTOOD."

**THOMAS BOSWELL**

# WHY IS THE AWARD FOR BEST PITCHER IN EACH LEAGUE CALLED THE CY YOUNG AWARD?

Each year, the Cy Young Award is presented to the best pitcher in the National League and the best pitcher in the American League. Why is such a distinguished honor named for a hurler who began his big-league career more than a century ago?

One quick survey of his record should be enough to convince any doubters.

Denton True "Cy" Young pitched in the major leagues from 1890 to 1911, amassing a record 511 wins along the way. The Ohio native was a member of the Boston Americans (later Red Sox) team that won the first World Series in 1903.

To commemorate the inaugural Fall Classic, in 1993 Northeastern University erected a statue of Cy Young on its campus, on the site of the pitcher's mound of the former Huntington Avenue Grounds, where the team played from 1901 through 1911, until moving to Fenway Park.

CY YOUNG IN 1905.

Young got his nickname while pitching for a minor-league team in Canton, Ohio, because his fastball damaged the wooden fences surrounding the grandstands in such a way that it looked as though a cyclone had hit them. Reporters shortened his nickname to "Cy," which was how he referred to himself for the remainder of his life.

Prior to his 1902 season with the Americans, Young, who had dropped out of school after the sixth grade to work on his family farm, briefly became the pitching coach at Harvard University. The sophisticated Boston newspapers had a field day with the incongruity of a sixth-grade dropout teaching Harvard men.

Cy Young was inducted into the Hall of Fame in 1937 (the second year of player inductions) along with Nap Lajoie and Tris Speaker.

# WHY IS MLB'S AWARD FOR COMMUNITY SERVICE CALLED THE ROBERTO CLEMENTE AWARD?

The Roberto Clemente Award is given annually to the MLB player who "best exemplifies the game of baseball, sportsmanship, community involvement and the individual's contribution to his team." With input from fans, each team chooses a nominee during the regular season. A panel of baseball dignitaries selects one winner from among the 30 nominees, and the winner is presented with the award during the World Series.

Known originally as the Commissioner's Award, it was renamed in 1973 following Clemente's tragic death in a plane crash on December 31, 1972, off the coast of Puerto Rico, while he was attempting to deliver supplies to earthquake victims in Nicaragua.

Willie Mays was the award's first winner.

# WHY DID THE HALL OF FAME WAIVE THE TRADITIONAL FIVE-YEAR WAITING PERIOD FOR INDUCTION FOR LOU GEHRIG AND ROBERTO CLEMENTE?

Because of their early deaths and their impressive on-field accomplishments, the National Baseball Hall of Fame made an exception to its induction rules for these two notable players: Lou Gehrig and Roberto Clemente.

Henry Louis Gehrig, famed first baseman for the New York Yankees, retired from baseball in June 1939 after receiving a diagnosis of amyotrophic lateral sclerosis. Six months later the Baseball Writers' Association of America held a special election to send Gehrig to the Hall of Fame, knowing he would not live long. He died in June 1941.

Roberto Enrique Clemente Walker was inducted into the Hall of Fame in 1973, just after his tragic death in a plane crash. He was the first Latin American and Caribbean player to be enshrined. His untimely death helped establish a new rule: a player who has been deceased for at least six months is eligible for entry into the Hall of Fame.

# WHY DO TEAMS PLAY "TAKE ME OUT TO THE BALLGAME" DURING THE SEVENTH-INNING STRETCH?

Although the seventh-inning stretch dates back to 1910, singing "Take Me Out to the Ballgame" during that break in the action began later—a high school game in 1934 in Los Angeles and later in the same year during the fourth game of the World Series, with the Cardinals and the Tigers battling for baseball supremacy.

The song gained its greatest acceptance in the 1970s thanks to White Sox broadcaster Harry Caray, who would sing the song to himself. Bill Veeck, the team's owner and master promoter, turned on Caray's microphone so that fans in the stands could hear him sing in his unique off-key style, and they began to sing along.

When Caray moved across town to call Cubs games in the early 1980s, his rendition of baseball's unofficial national anthem became even more popular, with various celebrities

FAMED CUBS BROADCASTER HARRY CARAY IS REMEMBERED IN THIS STATUE
OUTSIDE OF WRIGLEY FIELD IN CHICAGO.

invited to join in the fun. Actor Bill Murray was foremost among them.

The text for "Take Me Out to the Ballgame" was written in 1908 by Jack Norworth; Albert Von Tilzer added the melody.

The song was first sung in public by Norworth's wife, singer Nora Bayes, and became popular with many vaudeville acts. The couple was renowned for writing and performing other hits, including "Shine On, Harvest Moon."

Ironically, neither Norworth nor Von Tilzer saw a MLB baseball game until years later.

**"YOU COULD BE A KID FOR AS LONG AS YOU WANT WHEN YOU PLAY BASEBALL."**

CAL RIPKEN JR.

# WHY DO TEAMS PLAY THE NATIONAL ANTHEM BEFORE THE START OF A GAME?

"The Star-Spangled Banner" was written by Francis Scott Key, a lawyer, author, and poet from Frederick, Maryland, in 1814, the morning after he observed a battle at Fort McHenry in Baltimore during the War of 1812. The words of Key's poem were later set to an English drinking song and became America's unofficial national anthem in 1916, when President Woodrow Wilson ordered its use at military and other national ceremonies. In 1931, a congressional resolution made it the nation's official anthem.

When the country entered World War I in 1917, a wave of patriotism swept through the land. During the seventh-inning stretch of Game 1 of the 1918 World Series between the Chicago Cubs and the Boston Red Sox at Wrigley Field, players stood at attention, faced the center field flagpole, and began singing the song. The crowd, already on its collective feet, began to sing along and robustly applauded at the end.

Given the crowd's positive reaction, the band played the same song during the next two games. When the Series shifted to Fenway Park, Red Sox owner Harry Frazee, who several years later would authorize the infamous trade of his best pitcher, Babe Ruth, hired a band to play the song before the start of each subsequent game.

Following the Great War, and in the succeeding decades, the song continued to be played at baseball games on special occasions such as Opening Day, national holidays, and World Series games.

During World War II, baseball games became venues for grand displays of patriotism, which included the singing of "The Star-Spangled Banner" before games. By the end of the war, singing the national anthem became standard practice and spread to other sports. Major League Baseball currently does not have an official policy on how or whether players observe the anthem.

**"NO ONE'S GONNA GIVE A DAMN IN JULY IF YOU LOST A GAME IN MARCH."**

EARL WEAVER

# WHY ARE HOT DOGS AND BEER PERHAPS THE MOST POPULAR BALLPARK FOODS?

The short answer to this question is three-fold: they're easy to serve, they taste good, and they are easy to consume in the stands.

Two men get credit for introducing baseball fans to hot dogs. Some people point to a German immigrant, Chris Von der Ahe, who in 1893 began to sell sausages in buns at Sportsman's Park, the stadium that he owned in St. Louis, which was the home field for the Brown Stockings of the old American Association, a forerunner to the present-day Cardinals.

Others name Harry Stevens, a British-born entrepreneur who settled in Ohio and later moved to New York City, as the first to sell a "dachshund sausage" in a bun, which Stevens introduced at a 1901 Giants game when it was too cold outside to sell ice cream. A cartoonist covering the event was unable to spell "dachshund" and captioned his cartoon "hot dog" after hearing vendors shout, "They're red hot! Get your dachshund sausages while they're red hot!"

Beer was the type of refreshment available at ballparks. It was the most popular beverage in the Midwest among German immigrants, who would quaff suds during games while rooting for the home team. Credit for making beer available to fans goes to none other than the aforementioned Von der Ahe. In 1882, he cut his admission fee to a quarter and created a beer garden to get fans to spend more money in the ballpark than they would have otherwise. The strategy worked.

The American Association was often dubbed the "beer and whisky league" by its detractors, who thought it improper to sell alcoholic beverages at sporting events; the more established National League disdained this practice.

Except for the period in US history known as Prohibition (1920–1933), beer and baseball have been closely linked.

For decades, breweries were the principal sponsors of teams' radio and television broadcasts. Beer advertisements were prominent on many scoreboards and outdoor fences. Several men who owned breweries were also team owners, including Colonel Jacob Ruppert (Yankees), August Anheuser "Gussie" Busch Jr. (Cardinals), and Jerold Hoffberger (Orioles). Labatt Brewing Company was the original owner of the Blue Jays before selling the team to Rogers Communications in 2000.

Today, associations involving breweries and teams are exemplified by ballpark names: Coors Field in Denver, Miller Park in Milwaukee (which will become American Family Insurance Park in 2021), and Busch Stadium in St. Louis, which will remain so named until 2026.

"IF YOU WANT TO SEE A BUNCH OF HAPPY AMERICANS, GO OUT TO OPENING DAY AT ANY BASEBALL STADIUM IN THE LAND."

**BEN FOUNTAIN**

# WHY DID THE ATLANTA BRAVES LEAVE TURNER FIELD AFTER ONLY 30 YEARS FOR SUNTRUST PARK?

Moving from the familiar turf of Turner Field to a new stadium 13 miles northwest of the city was an unconventional decision in the minds of many fans in Atlanta.

Why did the Braves do it? One motivation was the fact that Turner Field was showing a lot of wear and tear. Another was the fact that during the previous 15 years, market research revealed that the majority of Braves fans lived north of the city's downtown area, where Turner Field was located. Finally, Cobb County officials made a sweetheart deal with the team by promising $400 million in taxpayer funds toward construction costs for the new site.

Did the 2017 move put more fans in seats? That's still debatable. During the first two seasons SunTrust Park attendance numbers increased slightly, as one would expect from the novelty of watching baseball at a new facility. Only time

TURNER FIELD IN 2013, BEFORE THE ATLANTA BRAVES ABANDONED IT FOR SUNTRUST PARK.

will tell whether the improved on-field product and surrounding corporate development, called the Battery Atlanta, will generate more attendance gains.

As to the fate of the former Turner Field, Georgia State University converted the facility into its football stadium and is redeveloping the area by converting parking lots into a massive mixed-use project that will include an expanded university footprint, retail businesses, and residences.

# WHY DID THE CHICAGO CUBS HOLD SPRING TRAINING ON CATALINA ISLAND, OFF THE COAST OF LOS ANGELES, FOR ALMOST 30 YEARS?

From 1921 to 1951, except for 1942–1945, when travel was restricted on account of World War II, the Chicago Cubs conducted their spring training on Catalina Island, one of California's picturesque Channel Islands, located 20 miles southeast of Los Angeles. The team trained there because team owner and chewing gum magnate William Wrigley Jr. was instrumental in the island's development.

The move brought national attention to the island, which Wrigley had purchased in 1919. The team would arrive every spring on one of Wrigley's fleet of ships used for transporting tourists from the mainland. During those 27 seasons on the island, the Cubs had nearly 20 future Hall of Famers, including Dizzy Dean, Rogers Hornsby, Grover Cleveland Alexander, and Gabby Hartnett.

Also accompanying the team for a time was a young announcer named Ronald "Dutch" Reagan, who would leave the world of sports broadcasting for a career as a Hollywood actor and later ascended to a rather successful career in politics.

Why would the team choose to move their training site from this paradise? A spell of bad weather during the spring of 1951, including a rare snowstorm, may have played a role in convincing the team to train in Mesa, Arizona, starting in 1952.

"I DON'T REGRET FOR ONE MINUTE THE TWELVE YEARS I'VE SPENT IN BASEBALL, BUT I COULD REGRET ONE SEASON TOO MANY."

**SANDY KOUFAX**

# WHY DID THE RED SOX BELIEVE IN THE "CURSE OF THE BAMBINO" UNTIL WINNING THE WORLD SERIES IN 2004?

Why in the world would Boston Red Sox baseball fans actually believe for 86 years that their team would never win the World Series?

It all began in 1920 when owner Harry Frazee needed extra money to underwrite the expenses for a new Broadway show he was sponsoring. How did Frazee get the added funds? He unloaded the man whom nearly everyone in Boston considered to be the team's best player–pitcher George Herman "Babe" Ruth.

Why did the legendary curse persist? It wasn't an overnight development; several steps appeared along the way for Boston, including:

- Losing the 1946 World Series to the St. Louis Cardinals in seven games, highlighted by the Cards' Enos "Country" Slaughter scoring from first base in Game 7 on a weak throw from right fielder Johnny Pesky

- Losing a one-game playoff to the Cleveland Indians for the 1948 American League pennant
- Needing to win one of two games against the New York Yankees to capture the 1949 pennant and failing to do so
- Losing the 1967 World Series to the Cardinals in seven games after having finished in last place the previous year
- Losing the 1975 World Series to the Cincinnati Reds in seven games after a dramatic walk-off home run from Carlton Fisk in Game 6
- Blowing a 14-game lead in 1978 and losing a one-game playoff to the Yankees for the American League Eastern Division title
- Losing Game 6 of the 1986 World Series when first baseman Bill Buckner booted a routine ground ball that allowed both the tying and winning runs to score, then proceeding to lose Game 7 to the New York Mets
- Getting swept by the Oakland As in the 1988 and the 1990 American League Championship Series (ALCS)
- Losing to the Indians in the American League Division Series in 1995 and again in 1998
- Losing to the Yankees in the 1999 and 2003 ALCS, the latter capped by Aaron Boone's pennant-winning walk-off home run

MEMORABILIA FROM THE 2004 RED SOX WORLD SERIES CHAMPIONSHIP ON DISPLAY AT FENWAY PARK IN BOSTON.

In 2004, it appeared as though the curse would certainly continue as the Yankees held a commanding 3–0 game lead in the ALCS, but, to the amazement of the entire baseball world, the Red Sox won four straight games and proceeded to sweep the Cardinals in the World Series. The Sox also won the World Series in 2007, 2013, and 2018, thus further eradicating the Curse of the Bambino.

**"LOVE IS THE MOST IMPORTANT THING IN THE WORLD, BUT BASEBALL IS PRETTY GOOD, TOO."**

YOGI BERRA

# WHY DID THE CUBS BELIEVE IN THE "CURSE OF THE BILLY GOAT" BEFORE THE TEAM WON THE WORLD SERIES IN 2016?

There's one simple answer to that question: because the Cubs didn't win a pennant between 1945, when the curse began, and 2016, when the Cubs captured their first National League pennant in 71 years and their first World Series title in 108 years.

The curse got its name from William Sianis, owner of the Billy Goat Tavern, who brought his pet goat, named Murphy, to Game 4 of the 1945 World Series at Wrigley Field between the Cubs and Detroit Tigers.

As the story goes, fans sitting near the goat became offended by the odor of the animal, and Sianis was asked to leave the ballpark. The angry fan took his pet and yelled to the crowd, "Them Cubs, they ain't gonna win no more." A variation of the story is that the goat was refused admission

THE ORIGINAL BILLY GOAT TAVERN IN CHICAGO.

to the stadium despite the fact that his owner purchased a ticket for him, so Sianis tied the goat's leash to a stake in the ground and went to the game alone, clearly offended.

Over the years, the curse became the subject of many newspaper columns and articles. In 1981, Ron Berler of the *Boston Herald American* came up with a theory, called the "Ex-Cubs Factor," that a World Series team with three or more ex-Cubs on its roster had "a critical mass of Cubness" and was likely to fail in the Fall Classic. In 1986, Mike Royko took this a step further with his "Modified Cub Factor," hypothesizing that even one former Cub on a World Series team would doom that club to failure.

Oft-cited examples of the curse's effects include:

- The Cubs' end-of-season collapse in the race for the 1969 National League Eastern Division title, having been ahead of the second-place Mets by six games on September 1

- Losing the 1984 National League Championship Series (NLCS) to the San Diego Padres after being ahead by two games to none in a best-of-five series

- Losing Game 6 (and subsequently Game 7) of the 2003 NLCS to the Marlins after Cubs fan Steve Bartman prevented Chicago left fielder Moises Alou from reaching into the stands to catch a foul ball for an out

- Getting swept in the 1998, 2007, and 2008 Division Series

- Getting swept by the Mets in the 2015 NLCS. The Mets' Daniel Murphy was the MVP of that series, making him the second Murphy to keep the Cubs from winning a World Series.

# WHY HASN'T A PITCHER WON 30 GAMES IN A SINGLE SEASON IN MORE THAN 50 YEARS?

Since Detroit hurler Dennis Dale McLain posted a 31–6 record in 1968, no major-league pitcher has won 30 or more games in a season. That phenomenon is due to several factors.

Foremost among them is the lowering of the pitcher's mound from 15 to 10 inches in 1968 following what has been called the "Year of the Pitcher," when the Cardinals' Bob Gibson posted an overpowering 1.12 ERA and slugger Carl Yastrzemski won the American League batting title by hitting just .301.

Another factor is the expansion of the number of pitchers. Beginning in the 1970s, most teams increased the number of starters on their staffs from four to five, giving each starting pitcher about eight fewer starts per season than he would have had as part of a four-man rotation. Additionally, the increased use of relief pitchers reduces the number of wins starters accumulate because starters leave games more often when scores are tied or they are victimized by relief pitchers blowing leads late in games.

Since Denny McLain's 31-win season, which occurred 34 years after Dizzy Dean went 30–7 for the World Series–winning Cardinals, two men have won 27 games in a season: Hall of Famer Steve Carlton did so with the 1972 Phillies, and Bob Welch shined brightly for the 1990 As.

Given the mitigating factors in today's game, it appears doubtful that we'll ever see another single-season 30-game winner.

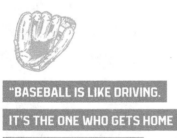

**"BASEBALL IS LIKE DRIVING. IT'S THE ONE WHO GETS HOME SAFELY THAT COUNTS."**

**TOMMY LASORDA**

# WHY HAS NO BATTER HIT .400 OR HIGHER SINCE TED WILLIAMS HIT .406 IN 1941?

When I was a preteen in Pittsburgh, my father gave me a pass to a box seat at old Forbes Field, where the Pirates were scheduled to play an exhibition game with the visiting Red Sox from Boston. Batting third in the BoSox lineup was, as expected, left-hitting Ted Williams.

During the pregame batting practice, when Williams stepped to the plate to take a few swings, a veteran fan sitting behind me tapped me on the shoulder and said, "Hey, kid, watch this hitter. You're gonna see the most beautiful swing you'll ever see in your life."

The fan's words rang with such authority that even a 12-year-old knew not to challenge his prediction.

Sure enough, he was right. It was as if the slugger's hitting coach was Fred Astaire and he could have performed that swing to a packed audience at Carnegie Hall.

Perhaps this was the secret behind Williams's uncanny ability to attain a .406 batting average in 1941.

Did Williams achieve this plateau of hitting prowess by virtue of his skill alone? Admittedly, skill was involved. After all, perhaps the most difficult task for any athlete is to face a big-league pitcher with the objective of hitting a round ball with a round bat.

But several other truths also play a part. The first is that pitchers today are bigger and stronger than ever before. Their fastballs are faster; their curves break more sharply. Also, because relief pitchers are called in more quickly, hitters are required to make more adjustments today than they were in Williams's era. "The Splendid Splinter" arguably faced lower quality pitching than today's hitters are required to overcome.

It is also worth noting that Williams hit .406 when MLB was six years away from breaking the color barrier. Pitchers today are selected from a larger pool of talent.

Williams arriving at that potent average did not come without a tough decision. The Red Sox were scheduled to end the season by playing a doubleheader against the Philadelphia Athletics. The 23-year-old was faced with a dilemma that had haunted him throughout the evening before.

On that final day of the season, Williams had technically not hit .400. His actual average was .3995. On the previous afternoon, his manager offered him the opportunity to

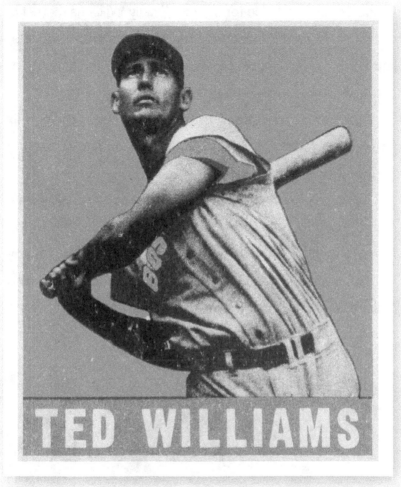

TED WILLIAMS, THE MAN WHO BATTED .400, ON A BASEBALL CARD FROM 1948.

take the final day off, since MLB rules would allow an official scorer to round up the numbers to .400.

It was decision time. According to Williams, he and a friend spent the wee hours of the night walking the streets of Philadelphia. Meandering for hours, they stopped twice for ice cream and twice for scotch. Finally Williams made his decision. He told his manager a few hours before the double-header that he would play. He would hit .400 legitimately, or not at all.

During the game, he did just that. In fact, he went six for eight, including a home run. His season-ending batting average was a whopping .406.

The closest anyone has come to matching Williams's record was George Brett's .390 average in 1980. Had the final two months of the 1994 season not been wiped out by a player's strike, Tony Gwynn might have equaled or even passed Williams's mark instead of finishing the truncated season with a .394 average.

**"IF I HAD KNOWN I WAS GOING TO LIVE THIS LONG, I'D HAVE TAKEN BETTER CARE OF MYSELF."**
**MICKEY MANTLE**

# WHY WILL ONE OF BASEBALL'S MANY RECORDS NEVER BE SURPASSED?

Throughout the century and a half of Major League Baseball, scads of eye-popping records stand out. They set standards toward which players strive. Sportscasters remind their audiences when one of those records is about to be tied or broken. Nerves rise when a home-run record is about to fall. People become excited when a pitcher's strikeout record is on the line.

But according to most analysts, there is one record that in all probability never will be broken. It was accomplished between May 15 and July 17, 1941.

The man who holds this eternal record is one of the icons of baseball. His name was Joseph Paul DiMaggio, and the *New York Times* called his hitting streak of 56 games in a row "perhaps the most enduring record in sports." Since pitchers are bigger and stronger nowadays, and relief pitchers are brought in more frequently to address certain game situations, the claim has some veracity.

An exaggeration? Maybe. But his hitting streak was amazing, of course. One of the phenomenal dimensions to this record is that after this streak ended, "Joltin' Joe" banged out another 15 straight games in which he hit safely.

DiMaggio enjoyed a storied career that set him apart from nearly every other baseball player in the nation. And, oh yes, he also married one of America's most beautiful women, Marilyn Monroe.

THE JOE DiMAGGIO PLAQUE IN THE BASEBALL HALL OF FAME.

# WHY DID A CHICAGO CUBS OUTFIELDER BECOME A NATIONAL HERO WITHOUT EVEN TOUCHING A BASEBALL?

On April 25, 1976, center fielder Rick Monday of the Chicago Cubs left the dugout to join his teammates during the first inning of their game against the Dodgers in Dodger Stadium. Little did he know that he would soon become a hero to fans from both Chicago and Los Angeles because of one patriotic gesture that fans still talk about today.

In the top half of the fourth inning, two spectators suddenly jumped onto the field and ran toward the outfielders, then dropped to their knees. The two men (who were later identified as a father and his son) took out a match and prepared to set an American flag afire.

While everyone in the stadium sat in shocked silence, Monday raced toward the two intruders, swooped up the flag (now soaking wet with lighter fluid), carried it quickly toward the Dodger dugout, and handed it to the Dodgers' starting pitcher, Doug Rau.

Several people in the stands, without hesitation, began to sing "God Bless America."

When Monday came to bat in the top half of the fifth, the partisan crowd gave him a standing ovation. The large scoreboard in left-center field flashed a reaction to what had happened just the inning before: "Rick Monday—You Made a Great Play."

In Monday's own words: "What they were doing was wrong, and I wanted them off the field. I didn't want them to be able to desecrate an American flag that some of my buddies lost their lives for."

Monday, who had served for six months in the United States Marines Corps Reserve, was presented with the flag a month later in a pregame ceremony at Wrigley Field by Dodgers executive Al Campanis as a gesture of patriotic pride.

Monday served 19 years as a big-league ballplayer with several teams. One fan asked him, "Doesn't it disappoint you, knowing that you spent 19 years in the major leagues and the only thing for which you'll be remembered is saving an American flag from being burned?" Monday replied, "You know what? That's not a bad reason for which to be remembered."

UPI Photo

If he's to be remembered solely as "the player who saved the flag" because of what he did in Los Angeles five months ago it suits Rick Monday of the Cubs, just fine.

# 'Flag-Saving' Rick Monday Will Long Be Remembered

**BY MILTON RICHMAN**
UPI Sports Editor

NEW YORK — (UPI) — From the moment he first set foot on a big league field 16 years ago, Rick Monday had a place in Cooperstown all set aside for him.

If he didn't make it into baseball's Hall of Fame itself, he couldn't possibly miss winding up in the Hall's library where they keep records and newspaper stories of those players with any distinction whatsoever.

In the 16 years he has been with the A's and Cubs, Rick Monday has been a good ball player. Maybe not a great one, but certainly a good one.

He won't get too many votes for the Hall of Fame when he's through, but he does have a spot in the library already guaranteed him as the first player ever selected in baseball's first free agent draft in June of 1965.

Those who like to dig back into baseball history always will be able to find the Cubs' 30-year old lefthanded hitter there for that distinction as well as for being a completely dedicated and dependable performer.

No matter what else he does though between now and the time he quits, Rick Monday always will be remembered as "the player who saved the flag," for, the rest of his life, even if he lives to be 200.

In his time in the majors, Monday has accumulated more than 1200 hits, driven in more than 500 runs and has hit more than 169 home runs, but if he's to be remembered henceforth and forever more solely as "the player who saved the flag" because of what he did spontaneously in Los Angeles five months ago, it suits him fine.

"That's not a bad thing to be remembered for," says Rick Monday.

The date was last April 26. The Cubs were playing the Dodgers in Dodger Stadium and Monday was standing in center field when two individuals, a father and his 11-year-old son, bolted out of the left field bleacher area onto the playing field carrying an American flag.

When they got to center field they spread the flag on the turf and the man reached inside his pocket for a cigarette lighter.

On the Chicago bench, some of the Cubs players couldn't believe what they were actually seeing.

"They got a flag and they're gonna try and burn it!" said catcher Randy Hundley incredulously.

The father and son were kneeling over the flag, and when Monday saw the older man putting the lighter to it, he instinctively sprinted toward them.

"In my own mind, I didn't know what I was going to do, boot them over or what," said Monday. "I was thinking more about the flag then I was about them. I thought they couldn't burn it if they didn't have it."

So Monday snatched the flag from the father and the son, kept on going and handed it to one of the Dodger Stadium ball boys for safekeeping.

There were 25,167 in the park that day and when they realized what had happened, they began booing the man and the boy who were apprehended by the park police.

Then they applauded Rick Monday. The organist struck up "God Bless America" and everybody joined in. You never heard so many people all singing in all your life.

The man who tried to burn the flag eventually got off with a figurative slap on the wrist, a $60 fine and a year's probation.

Rick Monday has received thousands of letters and none were negative, not one of them negative. He has been commended by President Ford, by Richard M. Nixon and by George Wallace among others.

"Frankly," he says, "all the accolades have been a bit embarrassing. I don't feel I did anything that millions of others couldn't have done. If what I did served as some thought of awakening, if it was an action that reminded some people 'yes, we do care' then that makes me more proud.

"What moves me most of all was a phone call I received from a 15-year-old boy a day or two afterwards. We were in San Diego and he called me from Los Angeles. He said he, his father and mother had been in the ball park and had seen what happened with the flag. The boy told me that an older brother of his had been killed in Vietnam, and that when his mother and father heard all those people singing 'God Bless America,' they began crying.

"He told me his father and mother never had been able to express the way they had felt before about his brother's death in Vietnam.

"He said on the way home they talked about how what had happened with the flag on the field had for the first time put some meaning in what their son had done. Bear in mind, this was coming from a 15-year old boy. He had taken the initiative in calling me. It was a very moving conversation and I have never forgotten it. I don't think I ever will."

185

# WHY IS A CLOSE FOLLOWER OF A BASEBALL TEAM OFTEN REFERRED TO AS A "FAN"?

The answer is rather simple. The word "fan" is merely short for "fanatic."

This simple explanation may or may not win a small wager for you at your favorite watering hole.

Good luck.

**"IF YOU DON'T THINK TOO GOOD, DON'T THINK TOO MUCH."**

**TED WILLIAMS**

# WHY ARE ENTHUSIASTIC BASEBALL FANS SOMETIMES CALLED "BASEBALL BUFFS"?

The term "buff" originated in the horse and wagon days when firefighters rushed to fight a fire that threatened to destroy a local home or business. When a warning alarm rang and a siren sounded, townspeople would chase after the rescuers, who were already racing to join local volunteers in putting out the flames.

A Boston newspaper once described these followers as resembling a herd of buffalos chasing the wagon. The term became part of the local jargon, and people shortened the reference to the madcap followers to "buffs."

Throughout the early part of American history, some of the nation's founders considered themselves to be unabashed fire buffs. Benjamin Franklin was one. Twentieth-century buffs included Oliver Wendell Holmes in Boston as well as Mayor Fiorello H. LaGuardia of New York City.

Sportscasters adopted the term to describe the aggressive attitude of earnest followers of a local baseball team who would do anything, it appeared, to win a baseball game.

Baseball buffs may relate to an early fire buff who rationalized his enthusiasm thusly: "I don't want anybody's house to burn down. But if yours does, God forbid, I want to be there to see it."

"LITTLE LEAGUE BASEBALL IS A VERY GOOD THING,
BECAUSE IT KEEPS THE PARENTS OFF THE STREETS."
**YOGI BERRA**

# WHY DO WE DESIGNATE A SUBSTITUTE BATTER IN A BASEBALL GAME AS A "PINCH HITTER"?

That's a rather strange term for anyone called upon to enter a baseball game as a substitute for another player. Especially since this substitution normally occurs during a critical point in a game.

Experts have debated throughout the years as to the origin of this term. Some say it has to do with a manager grabbing the arm of a player sitting on the bench and telling him to go onto the field in lieu of a teammate.

Most baseball encyclopedias reference the idea that a team may be "in a pinch" and need, at that precise moment, a strong hitter who has the potential to smack a long ball that can score multiple runs in a hurry.

The designation has been employed since 1906, but who used it first is subject to another debate between (you guessed it) the New York Yankees and the Boston Red Sox (then called the Pilgrims).

# WHY ARE PARTICIPANTS IN THE MAJOR LEAGUE ALL-STAR GAME SELECTED BY FAN VOTES RATHER THAN BY THEIR STATISTICS?

Each year, around the first week in July, representatives of both the National and American Leagues in Major League Baseball square off against each other at a designated ballpark. Participants are selected based not on their performances—who has set the records to date for home runs, batting averages, runs batted in, etc.—but by their popularity that particular season.

That criterion was first established in 1933, when the first All-Star Game was played in Chicago at Comiskey Park on July 6. It was part of the 1933 World's Fair during the city's centennial.

The concept of the All-Star Game came from the creative imagination of Arch Ward, sports editor of the *Chicago Tribune*. The game was intended to be a one-time event to help build morale during a time known as the Great Depression. The *Tribune* labeled it the "Game of the Century."

Ward insisted that the players for the contest be selected by the fans. It became a tradition from that day onward. An estimated 55 newspapers throughout the nation printed copies of ballots, and it was said that 49,000 fans would attend the game with as much as $45,000 collected at the gate, all of which would be given to charity for needy and disabled former Major League players.

Actual attendance was 49,200. Many more fans listened in via CBS and NBC radio, with announcers Pat Flanagan, Johnny O'Hara, Graham McNamee, and Hal Totten calling the action. John McGraw of the New York Giants took on manager duty for the National League squad, and Connie Mack of the Philadelphia Athletics steered the American League players.

The National League got a bloop from outfielder Chick Hafey in the second inning.

The American League scored first in the bottom of the inning when NL pitcher Bill Hallahan walked Jimmy Dykes and Joe Cronin. Later, winning pitcher Lefty Gomez singled home Dykes for the game's first run.

In the bottom of the third, following a walk to Charlie Gehringer, slugger George Herman "Babe" Ruth smacked the first-ever All-Star Game home run. That made the score

# Babe Ruth Furnishes the Punch to Put American League Stars Winner Over Nationals

## AMERICAN LEAGUERS WIN ALL-STAR GAME

### Ruth's Home Run With Gehringer On in Third Puts Nationals Away by 4-2 Score

## MULVEY BLOWS A FIVE-RUN LEAD

### Redlands Wins, 9-7—Kelly Gets Three Hits

## HIT FOR THE CIRCUIT IN ALL-STAR GAME

## RED SOX MADE A FINE SHOWING

### 12 Out of 19 Games Won on Recent Trip

## HELEN JACOBS ELIMINATED AS MRS MOODY MARCHES ON

### Former Player Loses to Dorothy Round in Wimbledon Tourney—Hilda Krahwinkel Bows to "Little Poker Face"

## "THEY GOT THE BREAKS AND WON," COMMENTS McGRAW

### Declares Ruth Marvelous—Fans Besiege Connie and Johns For Autographs

### THREE BOSTON STARS PROVIDENCE WINNERS

### RED SOX AT SEATTLE IS SOLD TO WHITE SOX

### CAMPELL PITCHES A TWO-HIT GAME

### WALSH'S DOUBLE WINS THE GAME

## BOX SCORE OF ALL-STAR GAME

## Major League Baseball

### YESTERDAY'S RESULTS

### LEAGUE STANDINGS

### TODAY'S GAMES

3–0. After walking Lou Gehrig, pitcher Hallahan was lifted in favor of Lon Warneke.

In the sixth, Warneke hit a blazing triple and scored on a groundout by Pepper Martin. The National League made the game even closer when Frankie Frisch clubbed a home run.

Cronin led off the bottom of the sixth with a single and went to second on a sacrifice bunt. Earl Averill's sharp single to center scored Cronin, making the game 4–2.

The National League looked as though it might tie the game when, in the top of the eighth, with two outs and Frisch on first, Hafey lined a bullet to right field that appeared to head for home run territory. But Ruth ran, jumped, and caught the ball over the outfield fence to prevent more scoring.

The American League won the game 4–2 and the bragging rights for one full year.

"PLAYING THE GAME FOR PAY—HOME RUN. TEACHING KIDS TO PLAY THE GAME—PRICELESS."

**JACK PERCONTE**

# WHY IS THERE NO SUCH THING AS THE "BEST GAME EVER PLAYED" IN MAJOR LEAGUE BASEBALL?

Major League Baseball has been around for 150 years. Across that span, certainly the conclusions to all of the games were different to everyone who viewed them. And "best" does not necessarily depend on who won the game. Most fans are more complex than that. Many factors in a game will make a difference as to how it is judged by fans. How was the hitting? The defense? The running? The managing? The risks taken? The last-minute heroics?

In short, rarely do two enthusiasts leave any contest completely agreeing that it was the best game they have ever seen.

But, I must confess that in my many years on this earth, there was one game that, in my opinion, stands head and shoulders above any other.

It was played on June 24, 1947, between the Brooklyn Dodgers and the Pittsburgh Pirates at Forbes Field. The Dodgers won the contest 4–2. Rookie Jack Roosevelt Robinson scored the tie-breaking run with his first-ever steal of home plate off pitcher Fritz Ostermueller.

Why is this, for me, the best game ever played?

The answer is simple: It was the first Major League Baseball game to which my father ever took me.

"EVERYTHING LOOKS NICER WHEN YOU WIN.
THE GIRLS ARE PRETTIER.
THE CIGARS TASTE BETTER.
THE TREES ARE GREENER."
BILLY MARTIN